Abortion Rates in the United States

D1478175

SUNY Series in Health Care Politics and Policy
Robert P. Rhodes, Editor

Abortion Rates in the United States

The Influence of Opinion and Policy

Matthew E. Wetstein

State University of New York Press

Published by
State University of New York Press, Albany

© 1996 State University of New York

All rights reserved

Printed in the United States of America

No part of this book may be used or reproduced in any manner whatsoever without written permission.
No part of this book may be stored in a retrieval system or transmitted in any form or by any means including electronic, electrostatic, magnetic tape, mechanical, photo-copying, recording, or otherwise without the prior permission in writing of the publisher.

For information, address State University of New York Press,
State University Plaza, Albany, NY 12246

Production by Cynthia Tenace Lassonde
Marketing by Fran Keneston

Library of Congress Cataloging in Publication Data

Wetstein, Matthew E., 1963–
    Abortion rates in the United States : the influence of opinion and policy / Matthew E. Wetstein.
       p.   cm.—(SUNY series in health care politics and policy)
    Includes bibliographical references (p.   ) and index.
    ISBN 0-7914-2847-8 (hc : alk. paper).—ISBN 0-7914-2848-6 (pbk. : alk. paper)
    1. Abortion—United States—States—Statistics. 2. Abortion—United States—Public opinion. 3. Public opinion—United States. 4. Abortion—Government policy—United States—States. I. Title. II. Series.
HQ767.5.U5W46 1996
363.4'6'0973—dc20
                                   95–2884
                                      CIP

10 9 8 7 6 5 4 3 2 1

For Paul and Kate Wetstein, and Cindy

Contents

Figures

Tables

Preface

Several months before her nomination to the Supreme Court in 1993, Justice Ruth Bader Ginsburg suggested that *Roe v. Wade*, 410 U.S. 113 (1973) was a case in which the courts prematurely entered a political dispute that was being resolved in the legislative bodies of the states. Ginsburg indicated that states would have gradually repealed restrictive abortion laws in the face of evolving public support for abortion (Sullivan 1994). Her thoughts suggest that if the Court had held back and not ruled so forcefully in *Roe*, much of the political fury surrounding the abortion debate for the past twenty years could have been avoided.

Yet *Roe* was handed down, and many scholars contend that it came as an endorsement of a liberalization process taking place in many states (Rosenberg 1991; Segal and Spaeth 1993; Craig and O'Brien 1993). Others have argued that the *Roe* decision came just in time and that without it, a set of widely varying abortion laws would have resulted in the United States (Garrow 1994). The differing views on the impact of *Roe* suggest that we still have much to learn about the influence this decision has had on political disputes surrounding abortion since 1973.

While many authors have focused on the impact of *Roe* on the politics of abortion, few have studied the impact the ruling has had on abortion utilization. In part, this book was written to get at the heart of this question: How did *Roe v. Wade* influence abortion utilization in the United States? It also was written to demonstrate the connection between public opinion and public policy dealing with abortion in the American states. It is rare for scholars in political science to focus on the connection between mass preferences and policy outcomes, although a number of recent works have turned to this issue. It is even rarer for the focus to be placed on the state level. In part, this is due to our continuing fascination with national politics and to the ongoing partisan struggles that occur in Washington, D.C. This book is intended to orient students and researchers back to the states for fruitful study of the connection between the mass public and policy enactment. Specifically, the research in this book indicates that state abortion policies closely reflect the preferences of the mass public and demonstrates a connection between state abortion policies and use of abortion services by women. Thus, public opinion within the American states can indirectly influence the behavior of citizens.

This book has several other aims. At one level, it is an attempt to portray the importance of policy evaluation as a field of study in political science. Readers can consider this book a quantitative case study of the consequences of policy change on the behavior of the mass public in one issue area, abortion politics. Along this line, significant attention is devoted to policy changes in the abortion field and the impact those changes have had on the availability and utilization of abortion services. The focus is on both national and state policy change. On the national scene, acts of Congress and Supreme Court decisions are analyzed to determine their impact on abortion utilization. The effect of state policy changes are also explored. At another level, the book employs a broad array of statistical techniques in the social sciences that can be used to examine public policies. While some readers might find the techniques difficult to understand, I have done my best to explain the need for such techniques and to account for the results in clear language. Moreover, I have compiled tables and figures to help crystallize many of the important points that emerge from the data. It should become clear that the various quantitative techniques used in this book are important tools that public policy researchers can use to understand the significant role policies have in the daily lives of citizens.

It must be stressed that this book is largely a quantitative exploration of abortion politics and abortion utilization. It does not contain any reference to the moral and philosophical debate that rages in our society over the practice of abortion. Students and researchers can turn to other sources for commentary on that debate. The focus here is rooted in the social science tradition of forming hypotheses, gathering data, testing hypotheses, and explaining results.

Acknowledgments

An author undertaking the task of writing a book accumulates a number of debts. I am grateful to acknowledge the following individuals for their aid.

A number of political science scholars were helpful in providing new insights on abortion politics and commenting on my work over the past five years. Michael Berkman graciously shared data on abortion interest group membership. Raymond Tatalovich provided encouragement and shared some of his research with me. I am one of many authors who have benefited from the ongoing research by Gerald Wright, Robert Erikson, and John McIver on the connection between public opinion and state policies. Several scholars gave me suggestions to improve my research at a number of professional conferences and in the informal "seminar through the mail" of the publication review process. For their comments, I would like to thank Susan Hansen, Glen Halva-Neubauer, Sam Patterson, Jerome Legge, Kenneth Rasinski, Dan Merkle, Sue Vandenbosch, Clyde Wilcox, Jim Bowers, Robert Lineberry, Ellen Dran, Malcolm Goggin, and Christopher Wlezien. Some of these scholars will see the impact of their work in the measures and data used throughout this book. Malcolm Goggin was gracious enough to review several of my research papers, and even more gracious to include one in an anthology of abortion research. The impact of his scholarship is evident throughout this study.

Portions of the data analyzed in this book were provided by the Inter-University Consortium for Political and Social Research. General Social Survey data were originally collected by the National Opinion Research Center at the University of Chicago. Data from American National Election Studies were originally collected by the Institute for Social Research at the University of Michigan. Data from the Illinois Policy Survey were collected by the Center for Governmental Studies at Northern Illinois University. I have also used data originally collected by researchers at the Alan Guttmacher Institute in New York, a nonprofit organization specializing in research in family planning issues. Staff members at the National Abortion and Reproductive Rights Action League also provided research publications that were pivotal for this study. Lisa Koonin at the Centers for Disease Control and Prevention also provided abortion data through 1992. Any errors involving the use of the data are solely the responsibility of the author.

This book was written over a four-year period while I was affiliated with three different institutions, which means that my list of acknowledgments is

ACKNOWLEDGMENTS

considerably longer than the standard one. At Northern Illinois University, I benefited from the advice and encouragement of many researchers and faculty members. I am grateful to Ellen Dran, a research associate at the Center for Governmental Studies, and Pete Trott, the director of the center, for allowing me to cut my teeth on public opinion research and for providing a supportive and collegial work environment. Craig Ducat donated his wonderful book on constitutional law, and set aside time to shoot the breeze across the hallway. Mikel Wyckoff was a quiet voice of support, humor, and a wonderful teacher of quantitative techniques. His knowledge and joy of teaching are reflected in the various statistical techniques that appear in this study. Lettie Wenner proved to be a concerned and timely editor when I asked her to review portions of the manuscript. Her assistance strengthened the quality of the writing and thought that went into it. Bob Albritton served as a mentor and friend over a number of years. Throughout our friendship, he represented the best of what a mentor can be, providing the right mixture of support, guidance, and camaraderie.

At the University of Evansville, I owe a debt of thanks to my colleagues in the Department of Political Science. Ron Adamson was a supportive chair who provided computer resources that went beyond the normal expectations of a junior faculty member. David Gugin, and several other colleagues, including Alison Griffith, Bill Pollard, Dick Connolly, Phil Auter, Doug Covert, Caroline Dow, and Matt Malek, provided weekly reality checks. Alice Jenkins gave tremendous secretarial support and participated in some of the data entry required for this study.

I also owe thanks to Cindy Ostberg and Jerry Hewitt at the University of the Pacific for allowing me to use computer resources to complete the book in early 1995. At California State University, Stanislaus, Steve Hughes and Debbie Little were instrumental in setting me up with computer resources at the final stages of this project, and Elizabeth Oseguera helped locate research material as my teaching assistant. At the State University of New York Press, Clay Morgan was kind enough to read the original draft of this manuscript and to find merit in its rough edges. He was timely in marshaling this manuscript through the publication process. I also am thankful for the helpful suggestions made to me by Robert P. Rhodes, the editor of the Health Care Politics and Policy Series published by SUNY Press.

A version of chapter 4 of this book originally appeared in an abortion anthology published by Sage Publications in 1993 ("A LISREL Model of Public Opinion on Abortion," in Malcolm Goggin, ed., Understanding the New Politics of Abortion, pp. 57–70). I am grateful to Sage Publications Inc. for permission to reprint that chapter here. I am also grateful to John Kincaid, editor of *Publius: The Journal of Federalism*, and Glen Halva-Neubauer for granting me permission to reprint a table that originally appeared in Glen Halva-Neubauer,

"Abortion Polity in the Post-Webster Age," *Publius: The Journal of Federalism* 20:3 (Summer 1990).

As is customary in any project, all of the colleagues previously listed bear no responsibility for crimes of omission or commission in this book. The responsibility for any errors, sadly, must fall on my shoulders.

1

The Link Between Public Opinion and Policy

The past decade has brought increasing interest among political scientists in abortion politics research. Yet, in a recent review essay on the abortion politics literature, Malcolm Goggin (1993, 22) suggested that a "number of puzzling and unanswered questions" about abortion politics "cry out for investigation." Ironically, Goggin's plea was grounded in a special issue of *American Politics Quarterly* that focused entirely on the politics of abortion.

Goggin specifically suggested that researchers begin to study the impact that shocks or interventions can have on public opinion and access to abortion (Goggin 1993, 22). For example, we know little about how the 1989 *Webster v. Reproductive Health Services* (492 U.S. 490) decision allowing states greater leeway to restrict abortion has influenced abortion politics and policy-making. Moreover, Goggin indicated that more research needs to be done on the impact policy can have on abortion rates in the American states.

This study seeks to address these concerns. Specifically, this book explores the variation in abortion policies that have been adopted in the American states. The impact policies can have on access to abortion and ultimately on abortion rates is one of the major components of this study. Likewise, policy interventions are explored to determine how policy changes have influenced abortion rates in the United States. Finally, this book presents research that for the first time connects public opinion on abortion with state policies on abortion and abortion rates.

Why Abortion?

The importance of studying abortion as a political issue should be readily apparent. No single issue has retained such a pivotal place in our political psyche since the Vietnam war. The two major political parties have staked out diametrically opposed views on the right of women to obtain abortion services (Tatalovich and Daynes 1981). Interest groups on both sides of the debate have fashioned rhetorical and symbolic arguments that strike at the core of individual values (Luker 1984). Even the labels that have been attached to the opposing sides, pro-choice and pro-life, point to the very different viewpoints individuals bring to the abortion debate (Luker 1984; Rosenblatt 1992).

Ultimately, the politics of abortion in the United States boils down to a number of conflicts at different levels. On the one hand, abortion can be seen as a religious conflict, pitting religious fundamentalists and strict Catholics against others in a moral dispute about the origins of life. Beliefs about life beginning at conception are pitted against secular notions of liberty and the privacy rights of women (Goggin 1993; Tribe 1991; Rosenblatt 1992; Petchesky 1984). Abortion has also come to represent a political struggle, with disputes over abortion policy filling virtually every level and branch of government (Goggin 1993). The issue has come to represent one of the most divisive topics for our Supreme Court, state courts, and political parties. Abortion clearly represents an ideological dispute as well, with most liberals endorsing the right to an abortion and most conservatives backing pro-life forces (Luker 1984; Petchesky 1984; Staggenborg 1991). Yet there are ideological divisions within each camp, with each side splitting between extremists who demand more direct action and less strident activists who pursue more reasoned means of persuasion and political change (Staggenborg 1991; Goggin 1993).

Perhaps one of the best ways to study abortion politics is to assess the nature and scope of conflict over the issue (Goggin 1993; Schattschneider 1960). Schattschneider (1960) has indicated that political disputes in the American system are often conducted between interests that have the most at stake, largely without public attention. It is only when interests begin to lose the political battle that the scope of conflict is expanded to include the mass public (Schattschneider 1960). Because attitudes about abortion are so intensely felt by partisans on both sides of the debate, minor losses often encourage those groups to expand the scope of conflict and call for public support (Goggin 1993). This was evident when pro-choice forces marshaled large demonstrations in Washington D.C., in response to the 1989 *Webster* decision.

Thus, abortion is an important issue to study because the scope of conflict over the issue is often altered by political decisions (Goggin 1993). When courts overturn or uphold abortion restrictions in the states, those policy decisions have the potential to alter political tactics at various levels (Goggin and Wlezien 1993). When legislatures and other policymakers alter regulations, the scope and nature of the abortion conflict is subject to change. Additionally, if public views on abortion undergo change, it is likely that the debate over abortion policy options will be altered.

Why Public Opinion?

Popular notions of modern democratic theory suggest that governmental policy will reflect the preferences of citizens (Downs 1957; Dahl 1956; Schattschneider 1960; Erikson, Wright, and McIver 1993). In the theoretical model of Anthony Downs (1957), political parties compete for the right to represent the mass public in the institutions of government. Thus, one of the mechanisms the mass public can use to shape or control policy is the ballot box. In a perfect Downsian world, public policy would reflect public opinion because political parties would have to pay attention to the aggregate preferences of the public.

Public opinion is often perceived as playing a vital role in our everyday notions of democracy. V. O. Key, in an often cited work, proclaimed that:

> Unless mass views have some place in the shaping of policy, all the talk about democracy is nonsense. (Key 1961, 7)

Key and other theorists focus on the boundaries that the mass public can set for policymakers (Key 1961; Schattschneider 1960). Such an approach implies that policymakers are given some leeway to enact policies on their own without having to constantly cater to the mass public. Yet if policymakers go beyond the contours of what is deemed acceptable by the mass public, they will be held accountable for their actions. This accountability is usually seen in the electoral process, with voters having the right to "throw the rascals" out of office.

Put simply, modern notions of democratic theory suggest that representation by elected officials is a crucial connection between the mass public and governmental policies. In shorthand notation, elected officials are supposed to represent the wishes of the public when they debate public policy alternatives. If officials execute their representative responsibility effectively, policies should resemble the aggregate wishes of the public.

Such a depiction of the connection between average citizens and public policy runs contrary to much of the recent literature in political science. Numerous authors contend that ordinary citizens have little influence over governmental policy. Scholars like Lowi (1969) and a host of interest group specialists (Schlozman and Tierney 1986; Cigler and Loomis 1986; Gais, Peterson, and Walker 1984) argue that government policy has become the domain of privileged interests in American society. Grant McConnell (1966) suggested some thirty years ago that private interests in our society have the power to capture policy domains and transform policy-making to their benefit. The predominant theme throughout this research is that the public interest, whatever that might represent, is rarely served in the formation of policy.

An example of this pluralist approach to policy formation might be found in the recent debate in the United States over health care reform. Although an overwhelming majority of the mass public supported some type of health care reform, the policy debate was dominated by special interest groups that were effective in defeating any attempt at reform. Here, mass preferences were outgunned by wealthy, privileged interests that were threatened by reform efforts. Rather than reflecting mass preferences, policy-making in this case reflected an elite-dominated competition between interest groups with the most at stake (Mills 1956; Dahl 1956; Schattschneider 1960).

It has also become accepted practice in the discipline to note the failings of the American public in educating itself on issues and the policy positions of candidates (Campbell et al. 1960; Converse 1964; Smith 1989). The American electorate is often uninformed, uninterested, and unwilling to tune in to many political issues. Voters are often perceived as having little impact on most important policy disputes—beyond the simple act of periodically electing government leaders. With an American public that appears uninformed and uncertain about the issues, it is difficult to make a connection between mass preferences and government policy. In the absence of a mass public connection to policy, groups and agencies with intense stakes in the outcome are seen as the major players in American politics (Dahl 1956; Buchanan and Tullock 1962). The result is that many have come to view our national politics as a system in which "minorities rule" (Dahl 1956).

The notion that politics in America is dominated by special interests is a recurring theme in political discourse. Yet, despite the apparent downfall of the rational man in democratic theory and the rise of interest group dominance, there are documented cases when policy does fall in line with the preferences of the majority. Wright, Erikson, and McIver (1993) have indicated that in state politics at least, states with more liberal public opinion tend to have more liberal policies. Their ongoing research on state public opinion has led them to conclude:

> State politics does exactly what it is supposed to do in theory—faithfully translate public preferences into broad patterns of policy outcomes. (Erikson, Wright, and McIver 1993, 245)

Thus, the ideological predisposition of a state's body politic leads to public policies that closely match those ideological leanings (Erikson, Wright, and McIver 1993, 252).

Robert Jackson (1992) has argued that state elections, political parties, legislatures, and interest groups should play a mediating role in the formation of public policy based on mass preferences. These institutions are supposed to aggregate the demands of the mass public and translate them into coherent policy alternatives. Yet his empirical study of forty-seven states suggests that there is a lack of "pervasive evidence that political system characteristics either promote or impede significantly the translation of citizen preferences into policy" (Jackson 1992, 45). Despite that finding, Jackson (1992, 45) concluded his study much in the same way as Erikson, Wright, and McIver (1993): "It should be stressed that citizen preferences are translated into policy." His research simply questions the extent to which political institutions alter or mediate the influence of citizen preferences.

Others have argued that policy preferences in the mass public have been remarkably stable on some issues, serving as an endorsement of government policy-making (Page and Shapiro 1983, 1992). Stimson (1991) has recently suggested that public opinion "moods" in the United States have followed patterns of policy-making on most issues. When the mood of the public is conservative, policies either reflect that mood or have anticipated it.

Recent work by Jacobs (1992a, 1992b, 1993) suggests that mass preferences on health policy issues helped American and British legislators enact national health policy reforms earlier in this century. Countering the pluralist school of thought, Jacobs has argued that "strong public sentiment produced weak interest group influence" in the development of the American Medicare Act (1965) and the British National Health Service Act of 1946 (Jacobs 1992a, 180). Because of widespread support in the mass public, government officials were able to downplay interest group demands and foster majority support for these programs by manipulating even higher levels of support in the mass public (Jacobs 1992b, 200).

The fact that research points to the connection between mass preferences and public policy may not be earthshaking news to some readers, but it does run counter to the literature of the past thirty years arguing that majority preferences hardly matter any more. In this spirit, we might expect public opinion on abortion to be an important guide for abortion policy-making. In states where mass publics are conservative on abortion issues, we would expect to find conservative abortion policies drafted by state legislatures and governors. Some researchers have already speculated on the effects public opinion might have on abortion decisions by the Supreme Court. Franklin and Kosacki (1989) have maintained that the Supreme Court's 1973 decision in *Roe v. Wade* was merely recognition by the Court that mass preferences on abortion were changing.

Abortion may be one issue area in which majority preferences play a large part in determining policies within the American states. One goal of this book is to determine what role public opinion on abortion plays in shaping state abortion policy. To a large extent, the study is a search for the connection expected by the conventional wisdom in modern democratic theory. Two major questions confronted in this study are: (1) What role does public opinion on abortion have in influencing state policies on abortion; and (2) How much does public opinion influence the number of abortions performed?

Why Abortion Rates?

Few studies explaining the variation in abortion rates have been presented in the literature (Hansen 1980; Tatalovich and Daynes 1989; Meier and McFarlane 1992, 1993). Scholars have been slow to move beyond studies of abortion policy to the next logical level: how policy affects abortion utilization.

The research that has been presented uses demographic and political variables to explain more than 60 percent of the variance in abortion rates. Yet the studies are flawed in two ways. First, no study of abortion rates includes a measure of public support for abortion. This is largely because data on abortion attitudes is hard to find across all fifty states. Instead, researchers have relied on surrogate measures of public support, like congressional voting on abortion (Hansen 1980). Second, reliable measures of state policy on abortion have not been used to account for abortion rates. Hansen (1980) used a five-point scale of pre-*Roe* laws to help explain abortion rates in 1976. More sophisticated policy measures have been introduced in the political science literature, but they have rarely been used as independent variables to explain abortion rates (Berkman and O'Connor 1993; Meier and McFarlane 1992, 1993; Goggin and Kim 1992).

Goggin (1993) has suggested that studies of abortion politics need to move beyond the use of policy as a dependent variable:

> Much research effort has been expended to try to explain variations in abortion policy across the states. Missing from the current agenda, however, is the use of abortion policy as an independent variable. Rather than sorting out what kinds of factors account for the degree of restrictiveness in state abortion laws, for example, there are a number of puzzling and unanswered questions about the effects of various policies that cry out for investigation: To what extent and in what ways does abortion policy affect abortion rates? (Goggin 1993, 21–22)

Goggin's plea is for research that moves beyond the doorstep of explaining variations in policy. Ostensibly, policies are enacted by governments to regulate the behavior of citizens. Scholars need to turn to the job of assessing the impact mass preferences and policy can have on mass behavior. It is precisely this issue that is addressed in the closing chapters of this book.

It is also important to examine abortion rates as a dependent variable to update previous research. Susan Hansen's (1980) study focused on abortion rates in the states just three years after the *Roe v. Wade* decision. Much has changed in abortion policy-making since that time, including a wider variety of restrictions at the state level and the elimination of federal Medicaid funds for abortion. An updated study of abortion rate variation might turn up new, significant factors.

Research Questions

This book explores a number of research questions concerning abortion politics. Many of the research questions are interrelated and ultimately are tied together to explain the variation in abortion rates in the American states. This section features a discussion of the research questions and the theoretical logic that drives them.

Theory testing in the social sciences begins with either an inductive or deductive process (Manheim and Rich 1986, 19). Hypotheses developed in this study emerged out of a combination of deduction and induction. For example, several years ago, an examination of abortion research and data indicated that more urban states had higher abortion rates (Henshaw and Van Vort 1988; Tatalovich and Daynes 1989; Henry and Harvey 1982; Hansen 1980). California and New York have consistently had the highest rates of abortion among the states. Thus, through a process of induction, the collection of a set of facts or evidence led to the generalization that states with greater metropolitan populations tend to have higher abortion rates.

That finding led to a deductive process that developed a set of theoretical generalizations. If urban states had higher abortion rates, there had to be other factors that would lead states to have higher abortion rates. For example, states with more liberal mass publics could be expected to have higher abortion rates, largely because the mass public would be more open to liberal abortion laws. States with liberal abortion laws could be expected to have greater access to abortion, making it easier for women to obtain abortion services.

A search of the abortion politics literature points the way to a number of previously documented hypotheses. Much has already been done in cataloging the variations in public opinion on abortion. For example, socioeconomic status of individuals has been shown to have a marked effect on attitudes toward abortion (Granberg and Granberg 1980; Ebaugh and Haney 1980; Legge 1983; Hertel and Hughes 1987). Wealthy and better educated citizens tend to have more liberal views, and respondents living in large metropolitan areas have also been found to be more open to abortion. Therefore, we would expect states with large concentrations of wealthy, better educated citizens living in urban centers to have more supportive attitudes toward abortion.

Religion clearly plays a large role in shaping the political climate of the American states. Daniel Elazar (1984) has maintained that each state has a unique blend of subcultures within its borders, depending on the political values of ethnic and religious groups that settled there. Throughout the debate on the merits of legalized abortion, religious group differences have existed in the United States (Cook, Jelen, and Wilcox 1992; Jelen 1988; Legge 1983; Ebaugh and Haney 1980; Granberg and Granberg 1980). Fundamentalist Protestant churches, Catholics, and Mormons have consistently been more opposed to legalized abortion than mainline Protestant denominations and Jews (Cook, Jelen, and Wilcox 1992; Jelen 1988). Because the American states are populated with varying degrees of these religious adherents, states are bound to have varying degrees of opposition to abortion.

All of these demographic factors—religion, education level, wealth, and metropolitan population—have a role in shaping aggregate public opinion within the states. Yet it has been difficult to find adequate public opinion data at the state level for the abortion issue. Wright, Erikson, and McIver (1987; Erikson, Wright, and McIver 1993) pooled a number of CBS News/*New York Times* surveys to create an ideological score for each state. Their research allowed them to demonstrate that states with more liberal publics tend to have enacted more liberal policies across a range of issue areas (Wright, Erikson, and McIver 1987; Erikson, Wright, and McIver 1993). Other researchers (Weber et al. 1972; Weber and Shaffer 1972) have used demographic variables at the state level to construct public opinion measures that match well with state policy enactments. Clearly, public opinion on abortion within the American states is subject to the unique population characteristics and environment within each state.

Demographic factors like the socioeconomic and religious structures can play a role in shaping the policies that emerge in the states. Berkman and O'Connor (1993) have indicated that financial contributions to pro-choice groups within the states can have a significant impact on abortion policies that emanate from state legislative chambers. States with greater pro-choice support tend to have more liberal abortion laws (Berkman and O'Connor 1993; Meier and McFarlane 1992, 1993). States with large concentrations of Mormons, as in Utah and Wyoming, have large Mormon representation in their legislative bodies, which has a dampening effect on pro-choice lobbying efforts (Witt and Moncrief 1993). The number of women serving in a legislature and their occupation of key roles can influence efforts to structure new policies on abortion (Day 1992; Berkman and O'Connor 1993). Strong financial support for a pro-life or pro-choice cause can be reflected in the number of satellite offices housed in each state (NARAL 1989, 1992). In short, the states are bound to vary in their interest group activity and legislative approach to abortion based on representation patterns, demographic structure, and public opinion differences.

Ultimately, these state differences translate into varying state policies on abortion. The devolution of responsibility to the states for abortion regulation through a series of Supreme Court decisions has brought forth a wide variety of state policies. Until recently, federal Medicaid money had been withdrawn from the policy equation, and states were free to use their share of Medicaid money to pay for abortions in any of seven circumstances (Weiner and Bernhardt 1990). These Medicaid guidelines ranged from paying for abortion on demand to paying only in cases in which a woman's life is in danger. Moreover, some states have been quick to challenge court rulings and to structure access to abortion around informed consent, parental or spousal notification, and waiting periods (Tribe 1991; Halva-Neubauer 1990; Craig and O'Brien 1993). Theoretically, these state policy differences can be correlated with the opinion climate, demographic makeup, and political environment of the states (Goggin and Kim 1992; Luttbeg 1992).

Judicial decisions like *Roe v. Wade* have had a profound effect on abortion rates in the states. Legge (1985) has demonstrated that the national legalization of abortion in the wake of *Roe* led to vast improvements in maternal and infant health in this country. The 1973 court decision brought on a large increase in the number of abortions performed in the United States (Hansen 1980). Halva-Neubauer (1990) has indicated that states differ in their approaches to court decisions, with some states active in bringing new challenges to the court while others acquiesce. Yet little has been done to chart the variation in state abortion rates through time series analysis, despite the clear intervention effect that can be modeled through the *Roe v. Wade* decision.

All of the previously mentioned variables have the potential to shape a woman's access to abortion. It is access to abortion providers that is the key factor in explaining abortion rates in the American states (Henshaw and Van Vort 1994; Hansen 1980; Tatalovich and Daynes 1989). Past studies have found a strong correlation (Pearson's $r = .72$) between the percentage of hospitals offering abortion services and the abortion rate within states (Hansen 1980; Tatalovich and Daynes 1989).

This study seeks to tie all these strands together in a full model that characterizes the variation in state abortion rates. The major hypotheses are outlined in table 1. A key contribution of this research is its inclusion of variables that have been omitted from previous explanations of abortion rates. Moreover, the connection between public opinion and public policy demonstrated by other researchers (Wright, Erikson, and McIver, 1987; Erikson, Wright, and McIver 1993), is likely to receive support from studies of abortion rates.

TABLE 1
Major Hypotheses and Research Methods in the Study

Hypothesis	Dependent Variable	Research Method
Changes in Supreme Court will lead to more con-servative rulings on abortion (chapter 2).	Index of votes on abortion cases	Guttmann scaling
Changes to less restrictive abortion policy will lead to increases in abortion rates (chapter 3).	Ratio of abortions to live births	Interrupted time series
States with higher socioeconomic status will have higher levels of support for abortion in public opinion polls (chapter 5).	Percent of respondents who support right to abortion	Multivariate regression
	Percent supporting govern-ment funding for abortions	
	Percentage opposed to parental notification provisions (1988–90 National Election Series Senate Panel Studies)	

Table 1 *continued*

Hypothesis	Dependent Variable	Research Method
States with more Mormons, Catholics, and fundamentalist adherents will have lower levels of support for abortion (chapter 5).	Public opinion measures from NES studies	Multivariate regression
States with larger urban populations will have higher levels of support for abortion (chapter 5).	Public opinion measures from NES studies	Multivariate regression
States with institutional variables that favor abortion rights (more women legislators, pro-choice governor, more Democratic legislators, and more abortion-rights supporters) will have fewer abortion restrictions (chapter 6).	Six-point index of abortion policy toward minors in 1992 Four-point index of Medicaid provisions for abortion in 1992 Ten-point combined index of policy	Multivariate regression
States with demographic variables that favor abortion rights (greater public approval, fewer Catholics, fewer Mormons, fewer Christian adherents, and higher socio-economic status) will have fewer restrictions (chapter 6).	Six-point index of policy toward minors Four-point Medicaid index Ten-point combined index of policy	Multivariate regression
States with greater access to abortion will have higher abortion rates (chapter 7).	Ratio of abortions to live births	Structural equation model using LISREL (path analysis)
States with fewer abortion policy restrictions will have higher abortion rates (chapter 7).	Ratio of abortions to live births	Structural equation model using LISREL (path analysis)
States with greater support for abortion will have higher abortion rates (chapter 7).	Ratio of abortions to live births	Structural equation model using LISREL (path analysis)

Table 1 *continued*

Hypothesis	Dependent Variable	Research Method
States with fewer Mormons, Catholics, and fundamentalist adherents will have higher abortion rates (chapter 7).	Ratio of abortion to live births	Structural equation model using LISREL (path analysis)
States with larger urban populations and higher socioeconomic status will have higher abortion rates (chapter 7).	Ratio of abortions to live births	Structural equation model using LISREL (path analysis)

Chapter numbers are included in parentheses to indicate where the results are presented in the book.

Organization of the Study

The research presented follows a sequence that builds up to a causal model of abortion rates in the American states. Chapter 2 presents a detailed account of the impact the Supreme Court has had on abortion policy since deciding *Roe v. Wade*. Specifically, the changing composition of the Court over time helps to explain the evolution of the Court from a largely pro-choice body to a sharply divided one that had fundamentally altered the meaning of *Roe* by the 1990s. In chapter 2, the notion of policy change is studied from the perspective of Supreme Court voting behavior between 1973 and 1994.

After a discussion of Supreme Court voting behavior, the impact of policy change on abortion rates is detailed in chapter 3. Two different levels of analysis are explored. First, national policy changes, represented by the *Roe* and *Webster* decisions, are used in an interrupted time series design to test the impact these decisions had on national abortion rates. Additionally, the impact of national policy changes in Medicaid funding and the impact of the Reagan-Bush era are explored. Next, a series of state policy changes are analyzed to examine the impact of state policy change on abortion rates.

Chapters 4 and 5 focus on public opinion and its role in the abortion policy domain. Chapter 4 outlines the structure and stability of abortion attitudes in the American public with an eye toward demonstrating that stable attitudes allow researchers to pool responses on abortion questions across many surveys. This is important because such an approach allows one to build aggregate mean scores of public support for abortion. The stability of abortion attitudes also has important ramifications for policymakers. Public opinion data on abortion for each state are presented in chapter 5 and are linked to state policies and state abortion rates.

Chapter 6 presents a more detailed account of abortion policy variation in states during the early 1990s. The statistical models in chapter 6 seek to explain the variation in state abortion policies toward teenagers and Medicaid guidelines for abortions. One model explores the influence of political institutions on abortion policy, using variables like gubernatorial support, legislative composition, and interest group membership to explain variations in abortion policy. A second model uses public opinion and demographic variables to account for variations.

Chapter 7 uses the results of previous chapters to present a causal model of abortion rates. Multiple regression and causal modeling techniques are used to assess the direct and indirect effects variables have on abortion rates. The final chapter summarizes the research findings and makes connections to modern notions of democratic theory discussed in the opening chapter. Finally, suggestions for further research are offered.

2

The Supreme Court and Abortion Policy

The history of U.S. Supreme Court decisions on abortion is a history of a politically changing Court and a continuing struggle to interpret *Roe v. Wade* as a constitutional yardstick for state and federal laws. Interest groups and state legislators have turned to the Court and tested the limits of *Roe*'s trimester framework allowing for abortion on demand in the first trimester of pregnancy; state regulations to protect the health of the mother in the second trimester; and state prohibition of abortion in most cases during the third trimester. The bulk of court challenges since *Roe* lie in the area of establishing how far states can go to protect the health of the mother and to promote the state's interest in childbirth. Of course, many would argue that these regulations were enacted after 1973 mainly to discourage women from obtaining abortions.

The result is that the Supreme Court has been forced to pass judgment on a wide array of legal codes dealing with the regulation of abortion (Craig and O'Brien 1993; Epstein and Kobylka 1992; Tribe 1991; Rosenberg 1991; Ducat and Chase 1992a, 1992b). The Court has been asked to rule on state mandated waiting periods, funding restrictions, informed consent guidelines, spousal notification provisions, parental consent and notification laws, viability testing, licensing requirements, state mandated record keeping and reporting of abortions, hospitalization requirements, laws pertaining to physician duties, and guidelines dealing with the disposal of fetuses. More recently, the Court has been asked to rule on the protest activities of pro-life demonstrators. Many have criticized the Court for stepping into an activist, legislative role. Indeed, Justice Antonin Scalia has been highly critical of Supreme Court decisions and in his 1990 dissent in *Hodgson v. Minnesota* wrote:

> I continue to dissent from this enterprise of devising an abortion code, and from the illusion that we have authority to do so. (110 Sup. Ct. 2961)

This chapter outlines the history of Supreme Court decisions on abortion since the *Roe* ruling. The focus is on the changing political makeup of the Court as it evolved from a largely pro-choice majority in the early 1970s, to a fractured court seemingly on the verge of overturning *Roe* in the early 1990s (Goggin 1993; Epstein and Kobylka 1992, 290–292). The first section highlights the issues the Court has decided in the wake of *Roe*. The second section focuses on the changing personnel on the Court and its impact on rulings. Specifically, Guttmann scaling is used to characterize the changing policy coalitions on the Court in abortion rulings.

Issues Decided by the Supreme Court After *Roe v. Wade*

Roe v. Wade

The decision handed down by the Supreme Court in *Roe* was several years in the making. It was in the summer of 1969 that Norma McCorvey, a carnival worker, claimed she was raped on her way back to a hotel in Georgia (O'Brien 1986, 23). McCorvey later sought an abortion in Texas and was unsuccessful in a state that prohibited abortions unless they were necessary to save a woman's life. McCorvey eventually was forced to give up her child for adoption and later joined a lawsuit challenging the Texas law, with Henry Wade, the district attorney in Dallas, representing the state (O'Brien 1986, 24).

Original oral arguments in the Supreme Court case were heard in December 1971. Sarah Weddington, representing McCorvey under the anonymous name of Roe, argued that a woman's right to terminate her pregnancy could be found in the Ninth Amendment of the Constitution, which reserves rights that are "retained by the people," or in the Fourteenth Amendment's protection of the right to "life, liberty, and the pursuit of happiness" (O'Brien 1986, 27; Tribe 1991, 262).

After oral arguments, Justice Burger maintained that the case had not been argued well (O'Brien 1986, 28). After conducting a poll of the justices, Burger was unable to tally up votes in any meaningful way, although Justices Douglas, Brennan, Stewart, and Marshall did maintain that the law was unconstitutional (O'Brien 1986, 29; Craig and O'Brien 1993, 18). Burger assigned the task of writing an opinion in the case to Justice Harry Blackmun, a relative newcomer to the Court, but familiar with medical issues from his experience representing the Mayo Clinic in Minnesota. Blackmun's original draft drew criticism from colleagues who sought to overturn the Texas statute, mainly because he was too cautious in his opinion. Blackmun emphasized the vagueness of the law, where others wanted to base the ruling on the Ninth Amendment's protection of privacy that had been established in *Griswold v. Connecticut*, 381 U.S. 479 (1965). Eventually, the case was held over for reargument in 1972 (O'Brien 1986; Craig and O'Brien 1993, ch. 1). By that time, Weddington was able to point out that the strict abortion law in Texas had forced more than 1,600 women to travel out of state to obtain abortions (O'Brien 1986, 31).

The logic of the *Roe* opinion was laid out in a trimester framework that attempted to balance a woman's right to privacy and the state's interest in protecting a woman's health in the middle and later stages of pregnancy, and the state's "compelling" interest in "protecting the potentiality of human life" in the late stages of pregnancy (*Roe v. Wade*, 410 U.S. 113). Thus, states were allowed to regulate abortion in the second trimester of pregnancy, as long as the regulations were related to the preservation and protection of the mother's health. At the point of viability (roughly the third trimester), the state's compelling interest in protecting potential life kicks in, and states were allowed to proscribe abortion, except in cases to preserve the life or health of the mother.

The Court's 7 to 2 ruling surprised many who believed the need for a second oral argument, and the long delay between oral arguments and the decision, signified a deeply divided court (Epstein and Kobylka 1992). Yet the delay merely reflected Justice Blackmun's attempt to draw together a solid majority in favor of the decision to overturn state laws prohibiting abortion. Blackmun faced difficulties in structuring the ruling around the trimester framework and in establishing the point of viability in a way that would satisfy all of the justices in the majority (Epstein and Kobylka 1992, 197–198).

Justices Rehnquist and White dissented from the rulings in *Roe* and the companion case (*Doe v. Bolton*, 410 U.S. 179 [1973]). Both claimed that the right to privacy, upon which the majority opinion rested, had no constitutional basis, and they believed the compelling interest standard invoked by the majority was inappropriate. In a joint dissent, Rehnquist and White expressed dismay over the "raw judicial power" that had been displayed by the majority in crafting an "improvident" decision (Epstein and Kobylka 1992, 198). *Roe*'s immediate impact was to invalidate the abortion laws of most of the states in the American federal system. Table 2 is a list of state abortion laws prior to the *Roe* ruling. In essence, only four states (Alaska, Hawaii, New York, and Washington) and the District of Columbia had laws that fit within the rubric of the *Roe* decision.

Thus, most states were put in the position of drafting new abortion laws that fit the *Roe* framework. Yet many state legislatures did not act and allowed 100-year-old laws to remain in their statutes, despite the fact that they were enjoined from enforcing those laws (NARAL 1989, 1992). For example, the Arkansas legislature has not repealed a pre-*Roe* law that imposes a $1,000 fine and imprisonment for one to five years for anyone performing an abortion. Courts have declared the law unconstitutional and have issued an injunction that prohibits its enforcement against physicians (NARAL 1992, 8; *Smith v. Bentley*, 493 F. Supp. 916, E.D. Ark. 1980).

Parental Consent and Notification

After *Roe*, state legislatures began to enact restrictions on abortion that sought to test the limits of the *Roe* framework. The first tough challenge brought by a state emerged out of Missouri. Revisions of the state's abortion laws in 1974 required doctors to obtain informed, voluntary consent from a woman

TABLE 2
State Abortion Laws Before *Roe v. Wade*

States Allowing Abortions:

For any reason	To protect the woman's physical and mental health	To preserve the woman's life and cases of rape	Only to preserve woman's life	Prohibited all abortions
Alaska	Arkansas	Mississippi	Alabama	Louisiana
D.C.	California		Arizona	New Hampshire
Hawaii	Colorado		Connecticut	Pennsylvania
New York	Delaware		Idaho	
Washington	Florida		Illinois	
	Georgia		Indiana	
	Kansas		Iowa	
	Maryland		Kentucky	
	New Mexico		Maine	
	N. Carolina		Massachusetts	
	Oregon		Michigan	
	S. Carolina		Minnesota	
	Virginia		Missouri	
			Montana	
			Nebraska	
			Nevada	
			New Jersey	
			N. Dakota	
			Ohio	
			Oklahoma	
			Rhode Island	
			S. Dakota	
			Tennessee	
			Texas	
			Utah	
			Vermont	
			W. Virginia	
			Wisconsin	
			Wyoming	

Sources: Craig and O'Brien 1993, 75; Hansen 1980.

seeking an abortion; required mandatory record keeping and reporting to a state health agency; required a married woman to obtain the consent of her spouse before an abortion; required minors to obtain the consent of a parent before an abortion; prohibited the use of saline amniocentesis as an abortion technique; and imposed criminal penalties on physicians who failed to protect the life and health of a fetus (*Planned Parenthood of Central Missouri v. Danforth*, 428 U.S. 52 [1976]; Ducat and Chase 1992a; Craig and O'Brien 1993).

The Court split on the various measures in the law, with a 5 to 4 majority opinion striking down many of the provisions. The spousal consent provision, the criminal penalties against physicians who fail to protect the health of the fetus, and the amniocentesis prohibition were struck down by a 6 to 3 majority. All nine justices agreed with the record keeping and informed consent provisions in the law, indicating that they fell within the *Roe* guidelines of protecting maternal health (*Planned Parenthood of Central Missouri v. Danforth*, 428 U.S. 52; Epstein and Kobylka 1992, 219).

Blackmun's opinion struck down the parental consent regulations, arguing that they represented a "third party veto" over the decision of a physician and a woman (*Planned Parenthood of Central Missouri v. Danforth*, 428 U.S. 74). Yet the majority was only 5 to 4 on this provision, with Stevens joining the minority of White, Burger, and Rehnquist. Stevens' vote was prophetic because it represented a willingness on his part to include parents in the decision making of minors about abortion, while he was unwilling to force married women into the same role with spouses.

More important, Stewart's concurring opinion on the parental consent law indicated a willingness to uphold such provisions if they provided a route for minors to seek relief from judges when disputes emerged between parents and the child. Such a "judicial bypass" outlet would be expounded by the Court in subsequent years (*Bellotti v. Baird*, 443 U.S. 622 [1979]; *Planned Parenthood Association of Kansas City v. Ashcroft*, 462 U.S. 476 [1983]; *Hodgson v. Minnesota*, 497 U.S. 417 [1990]). In Bellotti, the Court voted 8 to 1 to strike down a Massachusetts law that required parental consent for a minor to obtain an abortion. Writing for the Court, Powell stated that minors must have the opportunity to go directly to a court "without first consulting or notifying her parents" (*Bellotti v. Baird*, 443 U.S. 647). As he had done in *Planned Parenthood v. Danforth*, Stevens dissented, maintaining the important role parents should play in minors' decisions.

Two years later, the Supreme Court voted 6 to 3 to uphold a Utah law that required parental notification by a physician "if possible" (*H. L. v. Matheson*, 450 U.S. 398 [1981]). Three of the original supporters of *Roe* were in the minority (Blackmun, Marshall, and Brennan). Stevens, who had previously been alone on the Massachusetts consent law, was now joined by the *Roe* dissenters (Rehnquist and White), Burger, Stewart, and Powell. The key wording in the Utah law placed the decision to notify parents in the hands of the physician and did not make it mandatory—only "if possible."

The issues of parental notification and consent emerged much later with a vastly different Court. By 1990, Stewart, Burger, and Powell had been replaced by Sandra Day O'Connor, Antonin Scalia, and Anthony Kennedy. While Burger,

Stewart, and Powell had been reluctant supporters of abortion rights since *Roe*, the appointment of three conservative justices by the Reagan and Bush administrations swayed the Court's balance. Indeed, there was wide speculation that the Court had moved to an anti-choice majority.

Yet in mixed opinions in *Hodgson v. Minnesota* (110 Sup. Ct. 2926) and *Ohio v. Akron Center for Reproductive Health* (110 Sup. Ct. 2972 [1990]), the new Court upheld similar parental notice laws as the earlier Court. But the new Court relied on an emerging standard of review favored by Justice O'Connor. Using an "undue burden" test to gauge the constitutionality of state laws, the Court voted 6 to 3 to uphold a Minnesota law that required one-parent notification with a judicial bypass. Similarly, an Ohio law that required "timely" notice to a parent of a minor about an abortion was held constitutional as long as a judicial bypass procedure was open to the minor. Significantly, Stevens and O'Connor joined with the liberal wing of the Court (Blackmun, Brennan, and Marshall) to strike down a portion of the Minnesota law that required both parents be notified of a minor's abortion. In O'Connor's view, two-parent notification was an undue burden, while one-parent notification was not. Moreover, a forty-eight-hour waiting period for minors was also upheld as constitutional, because it provided a parent time to consult with the child, her physician, and family members, and promoted an informed choice by the minor.

The *Hodgson* decision drew biting criticism from Justice Scalia. He succinctly described the fractured opinions of the Court in his dissent:

> As I understand the various opinions today: One Justice holds that two-parent notification is unconstitutional [without] judicial bypass, but constitutional with bypass (O'Connor, J.); four Justices would hold that two-parent notification is constitutional with or without bypass (Kennedy, J.); four Justices would hold that two-parent notification is unconstitutional with or without bypass, though the four apply two different standards (Stevens, J.; Marshall, J.); six Justices hold that one-parent notification with bypass is constitutional, though for two different sets of reasons (Stevens, J.); and three Justices would hold that one-parent notification with bypass is unconstitutional (Blackmun, J.)....The random and unpredictable results of our consequently unchanneled individual views make it increasingly evident, Term after Term, that the tools for this job are not to be found in the lawyer's—and hence not in the judge's— workbox. I continue to dissent from this enterprise of devising an Abortion Code, and from the illusion that we have authority to do so. (110 Sup. Ct. 2961)

The position of each Justice on parental notification issues in *Hodgson* is shown in table 3. What is important to note is that the 1990 Court had essentially the same split as the earlier Court on these issues. Despite the changing personnel, there was a continuing willingness to let states regulate abortion for minors, as long as a judicial bypass provision was available.

TABLE 3
Supreme Court Positions on Parental Notification
in *Hodgson v. Minnesota*, 1990

Justice	Two-Parent Notice, No Bypass	One-Parent Notice, No Bypass	Two-Parent Notice, With Bypass	One-Parent Notice, With Bypass
Blackmun	U	U	U	U
Marshall	U	U	U	U
Brennan	U	U	U	U
Stevens	U	U	U	C
O'Connor	U	U	C	C
Kennedy	C	C	C	C
White	C	C	C	C
Rehnquist	C	C	C	C
Scalia	C	C	C	C
Vote	4–5	4–5	5–4	6–3

U = Vote to declare provision unconstitutional
C = Vote to uphold provision as constitutional

Sources: Hodgson v. Minnesota, *1990; Tribe 1991, 199-201.*

Government Funding of Abortions

In 1977, the Supreme Court decided three cases that centered on issues of government funding for abortions. In all three cases, the Court ruled in a 6–3 majority that state and local governments could not be forced to provide funds for abortions that were not medically necessary (*Beal v. Doe*, 432 U.S. 438 [1977]; *Maher v. Roe*, 432 U.S. 464 [1977]; and *Poelker v. Doe*, 432 U.S. 519 [1977]). *Beal* focused on a Pennsylvania state law that prohibited the use of Medicaid funds for most abortions. The Court essentially indicated that participation in the federal Medicaid program does not force states to provide Medicaid funds for abortions. Indeed, the majority opinion indicated that states have "a valid and important interest in encouraging childbirth" (*Beal v. Doe*, 432 U.S. 445).

In *Maher*, the same 6 to 3 majority argued that states do not violate the Equal Protection Clause of the Constitution when they provide funds for medically necessary abortions only (*Maher v. Roe*, 432 U.S. 464). The *Poelker* decision extended the same sort of logic to cities, allowing governmental agencies the right to prohibit the performance of elective abortions in hospitals that they operate (*Poelker v. Doe*, 432 U.S. 519).

A decision on federal governmental funding of abortions came three years later (*Harris v. McRae*, 448 U.S. 297 [1980]). In *Harris*, the Court upheld the constitutionality of the Hyde Amendment, which prohibited the use of federal Medicaid funds for abortions, except to save the life of the mother. Thus, by 1980, the Court had handled funding cases at virtually every level of government, ranging from city hospitals to state and federal levels.

The 1977 cases featured dissenting votes from the solid *Roe* camp of Blackmun, Brennan, and Marshall. Justice Stevens, who is often described as a maverick of sorts, sided with them in the *Harris* case in 1980 (Craig and O'Brien 1993, 241). Despite his appointment to the Court by Republican President Gerald Ford, Stevens has been one of the most liberal justices on civil liberties issues throughout the 1970s and 1980s (Epstein and Kobylka 1992, 14–15, 20).

Another federal government funding prohibition was upheld by the Rehnquist Court in 1991. In 1988, the Reagan administration altered regulations dealing with family planning clinics that provided abortions and abortion counseling (the so-called gag rule). The new regulations prohibited federal government funding at clinics "where abortion is a method of family planning" (Ducat and Chase 1992, 589; Trager 1993, 26). For three years, the regulations were prevented from entering into effect because of court challenges.

On May 23, 1991, the Court held in a 5 to 4 majority that the regulations were constitutional (*Rust v. Sullivan*, 111 Sup. Ct. 1759 [1991]). Using the same logic found in earlier opinions, Rehnquist wrote: "The government...may validly choose to fund childbirth over abortion" (Trager 1993, 26). O'Connor dissented in the ruling, but on different grounds than Blackmun, Marshall, and Stevens. O'Connor maintained that the Court should wait to decide on a case until it was justiciable, arguing that no one's constitutional rights had been violated yet. David Souter, the newest member of the Court, joined the majority in upholding the regulation.

Members of Congress responded to the ruling in *Rust v. Sullivan* by trying to overturn the gag rule and reinstate funding for the clinics in the Health and Human Services appropriations bill. When President Bush vetoed the bill, the House fell 12 votes short of overriding his veto (Ducat and Chase 1992b, 35–36; Trager 1993, 76). The regulations affected more than 4,000 family planning clinics across the country (Trager 1993, 26). One of President Clinton's first steps in 1993 was to rescind the gag rule that prohibited abortion counseling in federally funded clinics.

It is important to point out that funding restrictions at the federal level have consistently been supported by the Supreme Court since the *Roe v. Wade* ruling. No matter what the composition of the Court has been, Supreme Court majorities have upheld federal and state restrictions on funding of abortions that fit within the government's interest in promoting childbirth and protecting a woman's health.

Restrictions on the Performance of Abortions:
The Road to *Webster*

While *Poelker v. Doe* gave cities the power to prohibit elective abortions in city-owned hospitals, the Supreme Court has often taken a dim view toward regulations that impose restrictions on the physician's performance of abortions in certain locations and under specific conditions. Because of their vagueness, the Court has consistently overturned laws that require physicians to attend to the life and health of the fetus (*Planned Parenthood of Central Missouri v. Danforth*, 428 U.S. 52; *Colautti v. Franklin*, 439 U.S. 379 [1979]; *Thornburgh v. American College of Obstetricians and Gynecologists*, 476 U.S. 747 [1986]).

Restrictions on the place where abortions must be performed have met with mixed results in Supreme Court cases. In 1983, the Court overturned a law that required all second trimester abortions be performed in hospitals (*Akron v. Akron Center for Reproductive Health*, 462 U.S. 416). The opinion for the 6 to 3 majority indicated that Akron's requirement that all second trimester dilatation and evacuation abortion procedures be performed in hospitals:

> Imposed a heavy, and unnecessary, burden on women's access to a relatively inexpensive, otherwise accessible, and safe abortion procedure. (462 U.S. 438)

In a companion case, the Court overturned a similar requirement in Missouri that required all abortions after the twelfth week of pregnancy be performed in hospitals (*Planned Parenthood Association of Kansas City v. Ashcroft*, 462 U.S. 476). Yet an 8 to 1 majority upheld a Virginia law that required second trimester abortions be performed in licensed clinics (*Simonopoulos v. Virginia*, 462 U.S. 506 [1983]). The distinction in *Simonopoulos* appeared to center on a state's valid interest in licensing clinics and abortion providers after the first trimester, as well as a particularly gut-wrenching case dealing with a late abortion gone amiss.[1]

In the *Danforth* and *Colautti* decisions (6 to 3), White, Burger, and Rehnquist were in dissent. Burger's dissent is important because he had supported *Roe* just a few years earlier. It should be noted that Sandra Day O'Connor's appointment to the Court allowed for a 5 to 4 majority to uphold the presence of a second physician during post-viability abortions (*Planned Parenthood Association of Kansas City v. Ashcroft*, 462 U.S. 476). Obviously, the existence of the post-viability language made this regulation more acceptable than previous vague language that had come before the Court.

Votes by Burger and O'Connor also were important in upholding physician regulations in the landmark 1989 case of *Webster v. Reproductive Health Services* (492 U.S. 490). The ruling provided states a new opportunity to

---

1. The facts in the case centered on a physician who provided a late abortion to a minor who ended up discarding the aborted fetus in a hotel waste basket.

regulate abortion by upholding a sweeping set of laws in Missouri. Included among them were provisions that called for doctors to perform viability tests after the twentieth week of pregnancy before performing abortions; a prohibition of abortions by state-employed physicians in state-owned hospitals (unless to save the life of the woman); and a ban on state funds for facilities that counsel and provide for abortions.

Webster's importance lies in its clear abandonment of the *Roe* trimester framework. Borrowing language from previous dissents by O'Connor (*Akron v. Akron Center for Reproductive Health*, 462 U.S. 462), Rehnquist maintained in the plurality opinion that the *Roe* trimester framework was "unsound in principle and unworkable in practice" (492 U.S. 519). Scalia argued that *Roe* should be abandoned. In all, five of the nine Justices were now questioning the logic of the *Roe* trimester ruling: Scalia in an outright way; Rehnquist, with White and Kennedy, in a more muted way; and O'Connor because scientific advances were pushing viability forward (Blank 1984; Epstein and Kobylka 1992, 282–284; Ducat and Chase 1992a, 530–531).

It is no wonder that Justice Blackmun's dissent in *Webster* is so emotional. The author of the *Roe* opinion, Blackmun read his dissenting opinion in a somber tone that visibly displayed his distress (Epstein and Kobylka 1992, 282; Craig and O'Brien 1993, 232):

> Today, *Roe v. Wade*, and the fundamental constitutional right of women to decide whether to terminate a pregnancy, survive but are not secure. Although the court extricates itself from this case without making a single, even incremental, change in the law of abortion, the plurality and Justice Scalia would overrule *Roe* (the first silently, the other explicitly) and would return to the States virtually unfettered authority to control the quintessentially intimate, personal, and life-directing decision whether to carry a fetus to term...I fear for the future. I fear for the millions of women who have lived and come of age in the 16 years since *Roe* was decided. I fear for the integrity of, and public esteem for, this Court. (492 U.S. 538)

Blackmun was critical of his associates for questioning the constitutional foundation for the abortion right. While other justices, notably Scalia, pointed out that nothing about privacy or abortion could be found in the Constitution, Blackmun pointed out that many of the standards used by the Court could not be found in the text of the Constitution. For example, he wondered where the constitutional basis for the "actual malice" test existed (*New York Times v. Sullivan*, 376 U.S. 254 [1964]). Blackmun argued that the *Roe* trimester standard, like the actual malice standard, was simply a "judge-made method" of "evaluating and measuring the strength and scope of constitutional rights" (492 U.S. 540).

In the end, *Webster* opened a new era of abortion regulation in the states. In response to the ruling, eight states adopted new abortion restrictions by the end of 1991: Michigan, Nebraska, South Carolina, Mississippi, North Dakota, Ohio, Louisiana, and Utah (Craig and O'Brien 1993, 280; NARAL 1992). Moreover, access to abortion services began to shrink after the 1989 ruling. Data collected by the Alan Guttmacher Institute in New York indicate that 202 abortion providers closed their doors between 1988 and 1992 (Henshaw and Van Vort 1994, 105). The greatest decline came in rural areas, where hospitals increasingly opted out of the abortion business.

Yet four states liberalized abortion laws after *Webster*: Connecticut, Maryland, Nevada, and Washington (Craig and O'Brien 1993, 280–282). These states actually moved to codify *Roe* into state law, although through different means. For example, in Washington, state legislators had enacted a small number of restrictions after *Roe v. Wade*, including a parental consent law (NARAL 1992; Goggin and Kim 1992). Yet in 1991, a referendum on the Reproductive Privacy Act was adopted in Washington by a margin of less than 1 percent of the voters, guaranteeing a woman's "right to choose or refuse an abortion" (Craig and O'Brien 1993, 282; NARAL 1992, 130–131). The vote on the referendum was 756,812 to 752,588. Connecticut legislators passed a law in 1990 that codifies *Roe* into state law, with an added provision that requires minors under age sixteen to receive counseling, "including the possibility of parental consent" (NARAL 1992, 16).

The most important response to *Webster* came from Pennsylvania. Revisions of the state's abortion statutes there were passed by the legislature in 1988 and 1989, and signed by Democratic Governor Robert Casey. The new regulations imposed strict record keeping and reporting requirements on abortion providers; mandated a lengthy informed consent lecture and twenty-four-hour waiting period before an abortion could be obtained; established a new parental consent procedure with a judicial bypass; and required spousal notification for an abortion (NARAL 1992, 104–105; Ducat and Chase 1992b, 5; *Planned Parenthood of Southeastern Pennsylvania v. Casey*, 112 Sup. Ct. 2791; Slip Opinion 91–744 [1992]).[2]

The *Casey* decision is noteworthy for its extended discussion of *Roe v. Wade* as an important precedent that should not be abandoned. More than twenty pages in the opinion are devoted to *Roe*'s position in a long line of cases protecting privacy (*Planned Parenthood of Southeastern Pennsylvania v. Casey*, Slip Opinion, 1–27). Indeed, Justices O'Connor, Souter, and Kennedy state at several points that "the essential holding of *Roe* should be retained and once again reaffirmed" (*Casey*, Slip Opinion, 3). After several pages discussing the importance of precedent in maintaining the Court's legitimacy, the opinion

---

2. References to citations and quotes in the *Casey* decision are from the slip opinion. The published decision can be found at 112 Sup. Ct. 2791.

stresses that it is "imperative to adhere to the essence of *Roe*'s original decision" (*Casey*, Slip Opinion, 27).

O'Connor seems to have been the pivotal justice in ushering in a new interpretation of the "essential holding" of *Roe*. While the opinion in *Casey* reaffirms *Roe* as an important precedent, the trimester framework of the original decision is rejected (*Casey*, Slip Opinion, 30–31). The rigid trimester framework had long been criticized as unworkable in the face of changing medical advances, and the plurality in *Casey* merely eliminated that framework from the "central holding" of *Roe*. Instead, the Court recognized that states have an interest at any time during the pregnancy to promote childbirth and to promote informed and thoughtful decision-making by women (*Casey*, Slip Opinion 30–31). The key for O'Connor was whether state regulations to promote these interests represented reasonable interventions. If the regulations imposed an "undue burden" or a "substantial obstacle in the path of a woman seeking an abortion of a non-viable fetus," the regulations would not pass constitutional muster (*Casey*, Slip Opinion, 33-34).

Having reaffirmed *Roe*, while essentially changing its central holding, the O'Connor-Souter-Kennedy bloc went on to find most of the Pennsylvania regulations constitutional under the "undue burden" test. The only provisions the Court struck down dealt with spousal notification and record keeping provisions pertaining to spousal notification. These regulations were struck down largely due to briefs that indicated spousal notification would jeopardize the health and safety of many women who were in troubled marriages.

The informed consent lecture and twenty-four-hour waiting period in the Pennsylvania law were "reasonable measures" that did not represent "substantial obstacles" (*Casey*, Slip Opinion, 41–44). The Court maintained that these provisions might result in more informed, deliberate decisions about abortions and childbirth. Moreover, the one-parent consent provision did not represent an undue burden to minors as long as a judicial bypass provision existed (*Casey*, Slip Opinion, 57–58). All of these regulations won the endorsement of seven justices on the Court, with Blackmun and Stevens dissenting. All nine Justices upheld the definition of "medical emergency" abortions that had been drafted into the law. The votes to overturn the spousal notification provisions were 5 to 4, with the conservative bloc of Rehnquist, Scalia, White, and Thomas dissenting. Table 4 lists the splits on the various issues in the *Casey* ruling.

Several months after the Casey ruling, the Court refused to hear a case challenging Guam's strict abortion law (*Ada v. Guam Society of Obstetricians and Gynecologists*, 113 Sup. Ct. 633 [1992]). The denial of *certiorari* in this case drew a rare published dissent from Justices Scalia, Rehnquist, and White. They argued that portions of the law, which banned all abortions except in cases of medical emergencies, would likely have been upheld as constitutional. Therefore, they would have accepted the case, vacated the lower court's judgment,

TABLE 4
Supreme Court Voting in the *Casey* Decision

	Reaffirm *Roe v. Wade*	Medical Emergency Defined	Informed Consent, Twenty-four-hour Wait	One-Parent Consent with bypass	Spousal Notice
Blackmun	R	C	U	U	U
Stevens	R	C	U	U	U
O'Connor	R	C	C	C	U
Kennedy	R	C	C	C	U
Souter	R	C	C	C	U
Rehnquist	O	C	C	C	C
White	O	C	C	C	C
Scalia	O	C	C	C	C
Thomas	O	C	C	C	C

R = Vote to reaffirm *Roe*
O = Vote not to reaffirm *Roe*
C = Vote to uphold regulation as constitutional
U = Vote to overturn regulation as unconstitutional

Source: Planned Parenthood of Southeastern Pennsylvania v. Casey, *112 S.Ct. 2791 (1992)*

and remanded it back for further proceedings on portions of the law that passed constitutional muster (*Ada v. Guam Society of Obstetricians and Gynecologists*, 113 Sup. Ct. 633). The 6 to 3 decision indicated that, having decided *Casey* just three months earlier, most of the members of the Court were content to leave abortion challenges to another year.

Recent Abortion Rulings: Clinic Protests

Recent abortion rulings have shifted to the problem of abortion clinic protests, and the safety of clinic workers and women seeking services there. These cases have taken on significance in the wake of a series of shootings that have resulted in the deaths of several doctors and clinic workers since 1993. Pro-choice advocates have turned to two federal laws to attempt to prevent clinic protests, or to hold pro-life organizers responsible for financial losses and threats to the safety of people who work in and use abortion clinics.

The Supreme Court first ruled on this issue in 1993, when it ruled that a 100-year old civil rights law could not be used to bar anti-abortion protesters from blockading clinics (*Bray v. Alexandria Women's Health Clinic*, 113 Sup. Ct. 753 [1993]). In this case, operators of an abortion clinic in Virginia argued that organizers of a pro-life blockade had orchestrated a conspiracy to deprive women from using the clinic. Lawyers for the clinic maintained that this was in direct violation of the 1871 Civil Rights Act, also known as the Ku Klux Klan Act, a law originally designed to prevent organized discrimination against blacks in the wake of the Civil War. The six-member majority of the court held that there was no racial or class-based animus motivating the abortion protesters, and therefore the act could not be used to seek damages from the protesters. Justices Stevens, O'Connor, and Blackmun dissented from the ruling. They held that the purpose of the protesters was to conspire directly "to deprive women of their ability to obtain the clinics' services," and therefore, to deprive them of equal protection of the laws (*Bray v. Alexandria Women's Health Clinic*, 113 Sup. Ct. 753 at 799).

One year later, abortion clinic operators received a different ruling from the Court when it unanimously upheld the right of clinics to use federal racketeering laws against pro-life organizers (*National Organization for Women v. Scheidler*, 114 U.S. 798 [1994]). The Court widened the scope of the Racketeer Influenced and Corrupt Organizations Act (RICO), a statute originally drafted to combat organized crime and drug dealing. The ruling allowed abortion clinics to sue for damages against the Pro-life Action Network (PLAN) and a host of pro-life groups that had conspired to intimidate abortion clinic workers and prevent women from entering clinics for abortion services. The *Scheidler* case was the first abortion decision that Justice Ruth Bader Ginsburg voted on (Ginsburg had been President Clinton's first appointment to the bench, in place of Byron White).

Abortion supporters also hailed a 1994 ruling that upheld a 36-foot buffer zone that had been established around an abortion clinic by a local judge (*Madsen v. Woman's Health Center*, 114 Sup. Ct. 2516 [1994]). After repeated protests and arrests, the judge had enjoined pro-life marchers from approaching within 36 feet of the clinic, essentially forcing them to the opposite side of the street at the clinic's entrance and driveway. The judge had also enjoined the protesters from using loudspeakers and creating excessive noise between 7:00 A.M. and noon. Six members of the Supreme Court upheld these two restrictions on the protesters. However, the Court also held that an injunction against the display of images that were observable from the clinic was unconstitutional. Moreover, the Court held that the creation of a 300-foot "no-approach" zone, designed to prevent protesters from vocally confronting clinic workers and users was an overbroad restriction on the First Amendment right to free expression. A similar 300-foot zone around the homes of clinic workers was also declared unconstitutional (*Madsen v. Women's Health Center*, 114 Sup. Ct. 2516).

The pattern of voting in *Madsen* points to a six-vote majority that appears willing to protect clinics from overzealous protests by pro-life groups (see table 5). Justices Rehnquist, Blackmun, O'Connor, Souter, Ginsburg, and Stevens all voted to sustain the 36-foot buffer zone and noise restrictions. It should be noted that Justice Stevens even expressed a willingness to uphold the 300-foot no-

TABLE 5
Supreme Court Voting in the *Madsen* Decision

Justice	36-foot Buffer Zone and Noise Restrictions	Restriction on Observable Images from Clinic	300-foot No Approach Zone at Clinic and Workers' Homes
Stevens	C	U	C
Rehnquist	C	U	U
Blackmun	C	U	U
O'Connor	C	U	U
Souter	C	U	U
Ginsburg	C	U	U
Scalia	U	U	U
Kennedy	U	U	U
Thomas	U	U	U

C = Constitutional
U = Unconstitutional

approach zone at the clinic (*Madsen v. Woman's Health Center*, 114 Sup. Ct. 2516 at 2540). Conservative Justices Scalia and Thomas were joined by Justice Kennedy in opposing all of the restrictions on free expression grounds. Justice Scalia scoffed at the majority for upholding the noise restriction, pointing out that a videotape of protesters at the clinic demonstrated that pro-choice advocates were making more noise than the pro-life protesters (*Madsen v. Woman's Health Center*, 114 Sup. Ct. 2516 at 2547).

The Court's decisions have produced a long line of cases that largely shaped state regulations on abortion. Table 6 is a list of the cases in chronological order. From *Roe* in 1973 to *Casey* in 1992, the Court's composition had been transformed from a largely Democratic-appointed Court, and one that was expanding civil liberties, to one that was almost entirely appointed by Republican presidents. White was the only Justice remaining in 1992 who was appointed by a Democrat (Kennedy), and he was solidly in the anti-choice voting bloc. By 1995, Democratic President Bill Clinton had been able to add two moderate Democrats to the bench, Ginsburg and Breyer. Yet to claim that the Court moved away from *Roe* as the Court changed, it is important to examine the voting patterns of justices on abortion cases.

Supreme Court Voting on Abortion Cases, 1973-1994

For decades, scholars of the Supreme Court have been interested in the impacts presidents can have on the Supreme Court by filling vacancies with

TABLE 6
Abortion Cases Decided by the Supreme Court, 1973-1994

Case	Ruling and Vote
Roe v. Wade 410 U.S. 113 (1973)	Abortion left to judgment of woman and doctor in first trimester; recognized state interest in regulating abortion and protecting health of mother in second trimester; recognized state interest to promote human life and proscribe abortion in third trimester; 7 to 2 with Rehnquist and White dissenting.
Doe v. Bolton 410 U.S. 179 (1973)	Overturned hospital accreditation requirements, physician residency requirements, and requirements of committee or two-physician approval of abortion; 7 to 2 with Rehnquist and White dissenting.
Planned Parenthood of Central Missouri v. Danforth 428 U.S. 52 (1976)	State statutes requiring informed, voluntary, and written consent are constitutional; state mandated record keeping and reporting are constitutional; statutes requiring spousal consent and parental consent declared unconstitutional; regulations imposing criminal penalties on doctors failing to protect the life and health of the fetus declared unconstitutional; prohibition on the use of saline amniocentesis as an abortion technique declared unconstitutional; 5 to 4 with Stevens, White, Burger and Rehnquist dissenting.
Beal v. Doe 432 U.S. 438 (1977)	States not required to provide Medicaid funds for abortions if they participate in the federal program; 6 to 3 with Brennan, Marshall, and Blackmun dissenting.
Maher v. Roe 432 U.S. 464 (1977)	Equal Protection Clause of the Constitution not violated when states pay for medically necessary abortions but refuse to pay for elective abortions; 6 to 3 with Brennan, Marshall, and Blackmun dissenting.
Poelker v. Doe 432 U.S. 519 (1977)	Cities may prohibit performance of elective abortions in hospitals they own; 6 to 3 with Brennan, Marshall, and Blackmun dissenting.
Bellotti v. Baird 443 U.S. 622 (1979)	Parental veto of a minor's abortion unconstitutional without a judicial bypass option; 8 to 1 with White dissenting.
Colautti v. Franklin 439 U.S. 379 (1979)	Law requiring physician to be responsible for health and potential life of viable fetuses struck down as unconstitutionally vague; 6 to 3 with White, Rehnquist, and Burger dissenting.
Harris v. McRae 448 U.S. 297 (1980)	Prohibition of federal Medicaid funds for abortions other than to save the life of the mother ruled constitutional; 5 to 4 with Brennan, Marshall, Blackmun, and Stevens dissenting.
H. L. v. Matheson 450 U.S. 398 (1981)	Upheld state law requiring parental notification "if possible"; 6 to 3 with Brennan, Marshall, and Blackmun dissenting.

Table 6 *continued*

Case	Ruling and Vote
City of Akron v. Akron Center for Reproductive Health 462 U.S. 416 (1983)	Law requiring second trimester abortions be performed in hospitals ruled unconstitutional; parental notification provisions for minors ruled unconstitutional; informed consent guidelines mandated for physicians ruled unconstitutional; twenty-four hour waiting period ruled unconstitutional; guidelines requiring humane and sanitary disposal of fetus remains ruled unconstitutional because of vagueness in describing criminal conduct; 6 to 3 with O'Connor, Rehnquist, and White dissenting.
Planned Parenthood Association of Kansas City v. Ashcroft 462 U.S. 476 (1983)	Requirement that abortions after twelve weeks be performed in hospital ruled unconstitutional; requirement of a pathology report by the state upheld; a state requirement of a second physician's presence during a post-viability abortion upheld; parental consent requirement for minors upheld as long as a judicial bypass was available through a juvenile court; 6 to 3 overturning hospital requirement, with O'Connor, White, and Rehnquist dissenting; 5 to 4 in all other issues, with Brennan, Marshall, Blackmun, and Stevens dissenting.
Simonopoulos v. Virginia 462 U.S. 506 (1983)	Upheld law requiring second-trimester abortion be performed in licensed hospitals or clinics; 8 to 1 with Stevens dissenting.
Thornburgh v. American College of Obstetricians and Gynecologists (ACOG) 476 U.S. 747 (1986)	Overturned Pennsylvania laws requiring extensive lecture on fetal viability and risk of abortion procedure; intrusive record keeping and reporting provisions; a mandated waiting period for abortions; a second physician's presence when abortions are performed; and a statute outlining a physician's duty to protect the fetus; 5 to 4 with Burger, White, Rehnquist, and O'Connor dissenting.
Zbaraz v. Hartigan 484 U.S. 171 (1987)	Upheld a lower court ruling overturning a mandated waiting period; 4 to 4 with Burger, White, Rehnquist, and O'Connor "dissenting."
Webster v. Reproductive Health Services 492 U.S. 490 (1989)	No opinion on preamble of a Missouri law that finds life "begins at conception"; upheld restrictions on abortions in public hospitals by public employees only when a woman's life was threatened; upheld guideline that requires a doctor to perform viability tests after the twentieth week of pregnancy; upheld law that prohibits use of state funds to counsel women regarding medically unnecessary abortions; 5 to 4 with Blackmun, Brennan, Marshall, and Stevens dissenting in part.
Hodgson v. Minnesota 497 U.S. 417 (1990)	A two-parent notice provision ruled unconstitutional by a 5 to 4 majority, but a different 5 to 4 majority found a parental consent law with a judicial bypass provision constitutional.

Table 6 *continued*

Case	Ruling and Vote
	On the first issue, Rehnquist, White, Scalia, and Kennedy dissented. On the second issue, Blackmun, Brennan, Marshall, and Stevens were in dissent.
Ohio v. Akron Center for Reproductive Health 497 U.S. 502 (1990)	Provision that doctor provide timely notice to a parent of a minor seeking an abortion ruled constitutional if a judicial bypass option is open to a minor who can demonstrate mature judgment, parental abuse, or that the notice requirement is not in her best interest; 6 to 3 with Blackmun, Brennan, and Marshall dissenting.
Rust v. Sullivan 111 Sup. Ct. 1759 (1991)	Upheld law prohibiting use of federal funds provided to family planning agencies for the purpose of abortion or abortion counseling; 5 to 4 with Blackmun, Stevens, O'Connor, and Marshall dissenting.
Planned Parenthood of Southeastern Pennsylvania v. Casey 112 Sup. Ct. 2791 (1992)	Upheld a number of Pennsylvania restrictions, including a lengthy informed consent provision, a twenty-four-hour waiting period, state-mandated record keeping and reporting, and parental consent with a judicial bypass option for minors; overturned other restrictions, including spousal notification and records indicating spousal notification; stressed the importance of precedent and affirmed the "essential holding of *Roe*"; 5 to 4 with Rehnquist, Scalia, White, and Thomas dissenting.
Bray v. Alexandria Women's Health Clinic 113 Sup. Ct. 753 (1993)	Ruled that a Reconstruction era civil rights law could not be used by clinic operators to bar anti-abortion protesters from blockading clinics; 6 to 3 with Stevens, O'Connor, and Blackmun dissenting.
National Organization for Women v. Scheidler 114 Sup. Ct. 798 (1994)	Ruled unanimously that the racketeering statute (RICO law) could be used by clinic operators to bring lawsuits against pro-life groups that staged protests and blockades at abortion clinics.
Madsen v. Woman's Health Center 114 Sup. Ct. 2516 (1994)	Upheld a 36-foot buffer zone at the entrance of an abortion clinic and a restriction limiting the amount of noise protesters could generate at a clinic; overturned a restriction on the use of "observable signs" by pro-life protesters; overturned a 300-foot no approach zone near clinic and homes of clinic workers because they violated the First Amendment right to free expression. 6 to 3 with Scalia, Kennedy, and Thomas dissenting.

Sources: Adapted from Mezey 1992; Goggin 1993; Ducat and Chase 1992 1992a; Craig and O'Brien 1993; and Supreme Court decisions.

justices that fit their political views (Epstein and Kobylka 1992; Segal 1987; Tribe 1991, 167–170). Clearly the Republican administrations of Ronald Reagan and George Bush, through the appointment of five new justices, had an opportunity through the 1980s and early 1990s to transform the Court into an antichoice body. The analysis presented in the first half of this chapter suggests that there was a noticeable impact in at least three senses. First, there appeared to be a more fractured Court on the abortion issue in later years. Where a 7 to 2 prochoice majority had existed in *Roe*, the later years of the Rehnquist Court were highlighted by plurality opinions and divisive debates. Second, the Court had clearly moved away from the *Roe* trimester framework. Indeed, by 1992, the Court had essentially abandoned the trimester framework in the face of medical advances. Finally, the Court by 1992 had begun to rule much more in favor of state regulations, as long as they did not represent an undue burden on women seeking abortions. These findings suggest that a policy transformation had taken place in the Court's rulings.

Perhaps one of the most fruitful ways to examine the impact of the changing composition of the Court in an issue area is to use statistical scaling techniques (Spaeth 1963; Schubert 1963; Rohde and Spaeth 1976, ch. 4). Many scholars have used scaling techniques to assess the positioning of justices on a variety of cases. Comparing votes across a number of cases allows a researcher to create a spectrum of attitudes and values held by justices. Such an approach allows one to see the distribution of policy preferences that exist within the Supreme Court.

For instance, Spaeth (1963) used a form of Guttmann scaling to demonstrate the various positions of justices in the Warren Court on economic and business issues. Similar research has been done by Ducat and Dudley (1987) using principal components analysis to array the Burger Court justices on a continuum of pro-business decisions. Baum (1989) has developed a method of comparing justices across different Courts and has ranked justices on their support for civil liberties from 1946 to 1985. Baum's method allows him to identify Justice William O. Douglas as the most consistent supporter of civil liberties during that period, while William Rehnquist rated as one of the most consistent opponents of civil liberties (Baum 1989). Similar research has been done by Segal and Spaeth (1993).

Yet little has been done to assess abortion voting apart from other issues the Court faces (see Epstein and Kobylka [1992, 225] for an exception). Traditionally, abortion cases are lumped together with other civil liberties and privacy cases when researchers have been interested in examining the ideological distribution of justices (Segal and Spaeth 1993). Epstein and Kobylka's (1992) analysis of abortion voting through the 1975–1979 period indicates that Justices Blackmun, Brennan, and Marshall were solidly in support of pro-choice positions during that period (table 7). Outside of governmental funding and

TABLE 7
Voting on Abortion Issues Before the Court, 1975-1979

Justice	Overall Right to Abortion	Viability	Doctor Standing	Parental Consent	Government Funds
Blackmun	+	+	+	+	+
Brennan	+	+	+	+	+
Marshall	+	+	+	+	+
Stevens	+	+	+	−	−
Powell	+	+	−	−	−
Stewart	+	+	−	−	−
Burger	+	−	−	−	−
White	−	−	+	−	−
Rehnquist	−	−	−	−	−

+ indicates support for pro-choice position
− indicates opposition to the pro-choice position

Source: Epstein and Kobylka 1992, 225.

parental consent issues, the Court at that time had a majority of six votes that endorsed *Roe* (Epstein and Kobylka 1992, 225).

Epstein and Kobylka's (1992) analysis can be extended and improved upon. Their analysis focuses on issues rather than individual cases. An analysis of cases highlights a greater number of opportunities for variance in voting behavior. For example, although their table presents the positions of justices on selected issues, analysis of cases during the same period reveals eight different votes. Extending the analysis through 1981, the year O'Connor was appointed to the Court, ten cases are eligible for analysis.

Table 8 presents the voting patterns of individual justices on abortion cases that were decided by the Court between 1973 and 1981. The cases are arrayed in a continuum, with pro-choice policy decisions at the top (*Bellotti v. Baird*; 8 to 1) and increasingly anti-choice outcomes at the bottom (*Beal v. Doe*; *Maher v. Roe*; *Poelker v. Doe*; and *H. L. v. Matheson*, 3 to 6). The most consistently pro-choice justices are listed on the left side of the table, and the most anti-choice justices are listed on the right. Plus signs on the table indicate a pro-choice vote by a justice, while minus signs represent anti-choice votes. When a justice did not take part in a case, a zero is recorded. The scale of reproducibility listed at the bottom of the table is a statistical measure of the reliability of the voting patterns (number of votes that fit the pattern divided by the number of total votes). When the scale is close to 1.0, we assume that the voting pattern is reliable and that very few voting errors have taken place (here it equals .99). In table 8, there is only one voting error, when Justice Stevens cast an anti-choice vote in the 1976 *Danforth* case.

TABLE 8
Supreme Court Voting on Abortion Cases, 1973-1981*

Case	Justice									Vote
	Brn	Mar	Bla	Stv	Pow	Stw	Bur	Ren	Whi	
Bellotti v. Baird (1979)	+	+	+	+	+	+	+	+	–	8 to 1
Roe v. Wade (1973)	+	+	+	0	+	+	+	–	–	7 to 2
Doe v. Bolton (1973)	+	+	+	0	+	+	+	–	–	7 to 2
Colautti v. Franklin (1979)	+	+	+	+	+	+	–	–	–	6 to 3
Planned Parenthood of Central Missouri v. Danforth (1976)	+	+	+	–	+	+	–	–	–	5 to 4
Harris v. McRae (1980)	+	+	+	+	–	–	–	–	–	4 to 5
Beal v. Doe (1977)	+	+	+	–	–	–	–	–	–	3 to 6
Maher v. Roe (1977)	+	+	+	–	–	–	–	–	–	3 to 6
Poelker v. Doe (1977)	+	+	+	–	–	–	–	–	–	3 to 6
H. L. v. Matheson (1981)	+	+	+	–	–	–	–	–	–	3 to 6
Index of Support	1.0	1.0	1.0	.38	.50	.50	.30	.10	.00	

Index of support = number of pro-choice votes divided by total votes

+ represents a pro-choice vote
– represents an anti-choice vote
0 represents a justice not voting on the case

* Douglas is omitted from the table because he participated only in the *Roe* and *Doe* decisions.

Key to Justices:
Brn = Brennan   Stv = Stevens   Bur = Burger
Mar = Marshall   Pow = Powell   Ren = Rehnquist
Bla = Blackmun   Stw = Stewart   Whi = White

Scale of reproducibility = .99

Note that there appear to be three separate voting blocs on abortion issues during this phase of the Burger Court. Justices Brennan, Marshall, and Blackmun represent the liberal wing of the Court, with a 100 percent pro-choice voting record during the 1973–1981 period. Occupying the middle policy ground are Stevens, Powell, Stewart, and perhaps Burger. These justices tended to vote against the government funding cases, although Stevens did cast a peculiar vote in support of federal Medicaid funding in *Harris v. McRae*. Rehnquist and White clearly occupy the conservative anti-choice end of the policy spectrum during this period. Rehnquist joined a pro-choice majority once, when the Court struck down an invasive parental consent law with no judicial bypass provision (*Bellotti v. Baird*).

Sandra Day O'Connor's replacement of Justice Potter Stewart altered the balance of the Court on abortion issues (table 9). When Justice Stewart left the Court, he had been in the middle bloc of justices on abortion issues. O'Connor entered the Court and quickly sided with the conservative justices in a set of cases that spanned the mid-1980s. Justice Burger essentially moved over into the middle bloc, siding with the majority in overturning hospitalization requirements in *Planned Parenthood Association v. Ashcroft*. In all five of the cases heard during the 1983–1987 period, O'Connor sided with Rehnquist and White. In policy terms, the Court appeared to be divided down the middle, with a bare 5 to 4 majority through the mid-1980s.

The additions of four Reagan-Bush appointees (Kennedy, Scalia, Thomas, and Souter) and one Clinton appointee (Ginsburg) to the Court are reflected in table 10. Clearly the Court has become much more fractured in its rulings. Whereas the 1973–1981 period featured important cases that were largely settled by 7 to 2 and 6 to 3 splits (for example, *Roe, Beal, Maher*, and *Poelker*), the contemporary Court's major rulings have all been divisive 5 to 4 rulings (*Webster, Hodgson, Casey*, and *Rust*). Only the *Scheidler* case dealing with RICO's application to pro-life organizers drew a unanimous vote from the current Court.

The addition of new conservative justices moved O'Connor into the moderate abortion bloc, making her the often described swing vote on abortion issues. Note that her positions appear to have softened in reference to other members of the court, with 6 of 10 votes on the pro-choice side. The significant votes in *Casey*, however, come from two of her colleagues: Souter and Kennedy. Essentially, they represent the pro-choice votes in that case that had disappeared from the Court with the departure of Brennan and Marshall.

Comparing the justices across these three eras of the Court is possible if we combine the three tables and use the index of pro-choice support as a guide. Pooling all of a justice's abortion votes and creating a ratio of pro-choice votes over total votes, we can compare the justices on a scale of 1.0 to 0.0, with 1.0 representing the most supportive pro-choice Justices. Using the previous tables

TABLE 9
Supreme Court Voting on Abortion Cases, 1983-1987

Case	Justice									Vote
	Stv	Brn	Mar	Bla	Pow	Bur	OCo	Ren	Whi	
City of Akron v. Akron Center for Reproductive Health (1983)	+	+	+	+	+	+	–	–	–	6 to 3
Planned Parenthood Association of Kansas City v. Ashcroft (1983)	+	+	+	+	+	+	–	–	–	6 to 3
Thornburgh v. ACOG (1986)	+	+	+	+	+	–	–	–	–	5 to 4
Zbaraz v. Hartigan (1987)	+	+	+	+	0	–	–	–	–	4 to 4
Simonopoulos v. Virginia (1983)	+	–	–	–	–	–	–	–	–	1 to 8
Index of Support	1.0	.80	.80	.80	.75	.40	.00	.00	.00	

Index of support = number of pro-choice votes divided by total votes

+ represents a pro-choice vote
– represents an anti-choice vote
0 represents a justice not voting on the case

Key to Justices:

Brn = Brennan	Stv = Stevens	OCo = O'Connor
Mar = Marshall	Pow = Powell	Ren = Rehnquist
Bla = Blackmun	Bur = Burger	Whi = White

Scale of reproducibility = .98

TABLE 10
Supreme Court Voting on Abortion Cases, 1989-1994

Case						Justice							
	Brn	Mar	Bla	Gin	Stv	OCo	Sou	Ken	Ren	Tho	Sca	Whi	Vote
N.O.W. v. Scheidler (1994)	0	0	+	+	+	+	+	+	+	+	+	0	9 to 0
Madsen v. Woman's Health Center (1994)	0	0	+	+	+	+	+	+	+	–	–	0	6 to 3
Planned Parenthood of Southeastern Pennsylvania v. Casey (1992)	0	0	+	0	+	+	+	+	–	–	–	–	5 to 4
Hodgson v. Minnesota (1990)	+	+	+	0	+	+	0	–	–	0	–	–	5 to 4
Webster v. Reproductive Health Services (1989)	+	+	+	0	+	–	0	–	–	0	–	–	4 to 5
Rust v. Sullivan (1991)	0	+	+	0	+	+	–	–	–	0	–	–	4 to 5
Bray v. Alexandria Women's Health Clinic (1993)	0	0	+	0	+	+	–	–	–	–	–	–	3 to 6
Hodgsonb (1990)	+	+	+	0	–	–	0	–	–	0	–	–	3 to 6
Ohio v. Akron Center for Reproductive Health (1990)	+	+	+	0	–	–	0	–	–	0	–	–	3 to 6
Caseyb (1992)	0	0	+	0	+	–	–	–	–	–	–	–	2 to 7
Index	1.0	1.0	1.0	1.0	.80	.60	.50	.20	.20	.20	.10	.00	

+ represents a pro-choice vote

- represents an anti-choice vote

0 represents a justice not voting on the case

Table 10 *continued*

Key to Justices:

Brn = Brennan	Stv = Stevens	Ren = Rehnquist
Mar = Marshall	OCo = O'Connor	Tho = Thomas
Bla = Blackmun	Sou = Souter	Sca = Scalia
Gin = Ginsburg	Ken = Kennedy	Whi = White

Key to Cases:

Caseya = Votes to reaffirm Roe and overturn spousal notification provisions.

Caseyb = Votes to uphold informed consent, 24-hour wait, and one-parent consent with bypass.

Hodgsona = Vote to overturn two-parent notification provision.

Hodgsonb = Vote to overturn one-parent notification provision with bypass.

Scale of reproducibility = .97

as a guide, table 11 provides pro-choice "scores" for each justice that has served on the Court during the 1973–1994 period. Every one of the Reagan-Bush appointees has a pro-choice support score of .50 or lower. Indeed, Souter (.50) and O'Connor (.40) represent the only two consistently moderate members of the current Court. Four members of the current Court (Kennedy, Thomas, Rehnquist, and Scalia) have voting records that fall at or below .20 on the scale.

The recent departure from the Court by Justices Blackmun, Marshall, and Brennan left a vacuum on the liberal end of the abortion policy spectrum. Justice Ginsburg's expressed support of a woman's right to choose during her confirmation hearings, along with her first two votes on abortion cases, suggests that she will fill one of the roles left at that end of the Court. It is important to note that Ginsburg replaced Justice White, a consistent anti-choice vote on the Supreme Court, and readers would do well to view where each of those justices can be located in table 11. Interestingly, by 1994, maverick Justice Stevens found himself in the unlikely position of being the most experienced "liberal" on the Court when it came to abortion issues (.70). The Court's newest justice, Stephen Breyer, has yet to vote on an abortion case.

TABLE 11
Pro-Choice Voting Scores on the Supreme Court, 1973–1994

Justice	Ratio of Pro-Choice Votes	Total Number of Votes
Ginsburg *	1.0	2
Douglas	1.0	2
Blackmun	.96	25
Brennan	.95	19
Marshall	.95	20
Stevens *	.70	23
Powell	.57	14
Stewart	.50	10
Souter *	.50	6
O'Connor *	.40	15
Burger	.33	15
Kennedy *	.20	10
Thomas *	.20	5
Rehnquist *	.12	25
Scalia *	.10	10
White	.00	23

* Signifies current member of the Supreme Court (1995).

Justice Stephen Breyer is omitted from the table because he has yet to vote in an abortion case.

Perhaps the most telling statistic of the changing nature of the Court is a comparison of the average support score for the Burger Court of 1973 and the Rehnquist Court of 1992. The mean pro-choice support score for the *Roe v. Wade* Court was .63. The mean score for the *Casey* Court was only .35. The appointment of conservative, Republican judges to the Court by Presidents Reagan and Bush had the effect of altering the Court's support for pro-choice positions in a dramatic way. While *Roe* was reaffirmed in word by the *Casey* ruling, the actions of the 1992 justices, through their voting behavior, were far different.

The current Supreme Court, with two new Democratic appointees, may be rebounding back in the direction of the 1973 Court. The precedent of *Roe* is safer than it was three years ago. In short, the *Roe* ruling appears to have been saved by two trends: the apparent liberalization of Justice O'Connor, and the recent replacement of Justice White, a conservative anti-choice vote, with Justice Ginsburg.

While the composition of the Court has had an effect on the decisions handed down by the Court, there is considerable debate over the impact Supreme Court rulings have had on abortion utilization and state policy-making. Chapter 3 turns to this question, presenting mixed evidence on the impact *Roe v. Wade* had on abortion utilization in the U.S.

3

The Impact of Policy Change:
Courts and Legislatures

Little has been done to chart whether the Supreme Court's *Roe v. Wade* decision had a significant impact on abortion utilization. Although the number of abortions in this country clearly increased after the *Roe* decision (Hansen 1980; Legge 1985; Rosenberg 1991; U.S. Centers for Disease Control and Prevention 1991), time series analysis demonstrates that the landscape of abortion utilization had been altered prior to *Roe v. Wade*. In short, the trend of increasing abortions had been established before the 1973 ruling and did not dramatically change after it.

Such a finding is not news to abortion researchers. Susan Hansen (1980) indicated that the "largest increase in abortion occurred *before* the *Roe* decision, not after it" (Hansen 1980, 375; Segal and Spaeth 1993). Yet such conclusions have been made without the benefit of a time series long enough for the claim to withstand statistical tests. This chapter presents such a time series analysis, using data on reported abortions before and after 1973.

Research on the Impact of Abortion Policy Change

The literature on changes in abortion policy is a rich and expanding field of study. The field benefits from a number of disciplinary approaches and levels of analysis. This section highlights some of the important contributions that have been made by various authors.

Judicial impact studies are important because they demonstrate the role courts can play in policy-making, and they can characterize policy responses to court decisions. Johnson and Canon (1984, ch. 1) argued that Supreme Court decisions potentially influence four different populations: the interpreting population (lower courts), the implementing population (doctors and physicians), the secondary population (government officials, interest groups, and the mass public), and the consumer population (women with unwanted pregnancies).

In the spirit of judicial impact studies, Franklin and Kosacki (1989) suggested that the *Roe v. Wade* decision produced a small rise in public support for abortions that are necessary for health conditions. The decision had the power to boost public approval of abortion in cases of rape, possible birth defects, and when the mother's health was in danger (Franklin and Kosacki 1989). Yet, for abortions under other circumstances, Page and Shapiro (1992, 107) argued that support within the secondary population was polarized. Thus, "the net impact of the Court decision upon collective public opinion as a whole was negligible" (Page and Shapiro 1992, 107).

Other scholars have concluded that Supreme Court rulings on abortion have fostered greater interest group activity in the abortion arena, which suggests that court rulings have influenced other segments of the secondary population (Goggin and Wlezien 1993). A study of the South Carolina legislature in the post-*Webster* era concludes that the 1989 Supreme Court decision significantly altered pro-choice interest group activities in that state (Woliver 1991). An analysis of abortion rates in the wake of *Roe v. Wade*, which is presented in this chapter, attempts to assess the ruling's impact on the consumer population.

Canon (1992) has suggested that Supreme Court abortion rulings represent an example of the Court's potential to serve as a "cheerleader" in political and moral disputes in our country, attempting to sway adherents to the logic of its decisions. As such, Canon contends that the cast of cheerleaders on the Court was dramatically changed in 1986 and 1987 with the replacements of Chief Justice Warren Burger and Justice Lewis Powell by Antonin Scalia and Anthony Kennedy. He suggests that the Court "stopped booing and hissing the pro-life forces and began responding more positively to their challenges" (Canon 1992, 643). Court decisions like *Webster v. Reproductive Health Services* and *Rust v. Sullivan* did not represent radical policy changes, but the rationale and language that appeared in the opinions demonstrated that the Court had "crossed the playing field and [was] now shouting for the other team" (Canon 1992, 644). A conception of the Court as cheerleader seems to fit with Johnson and Canon's (1984) notion of court influences on a secondary public. But researchers are led to wonder whether the Court sometimes goes beyond the role of cheerleader and actually "suits up for the game" in political-moral disputes.

While some researchers have focused on Supreme Court rulings and their influence on abortion policy, others have focused on state legislative changes. Meier and McFarlane (1992) used pooled time series data over eight years to characterize the influences state variables can have on Medicaid funding of abortions. Their study of 1983, 1985, 1987, and 1989 data demonstrated that one of the most important influences on public funding for abortions is the overall Medicaid generosity of a state (Meier and McFarlane 1992, 694–695). Thus, states that have more generous Medicaid policies also tend to have more liberal Medicaid policies for abortions. States that funded abortions in the late 1970s also tended to have a higher probability of providing Medicaid funds for abortions. The number of National Abortion Rights Action League (NARAL) members within a state correlates with generous funding provisions, and the percentage of Catholic residents in a state correlates with more restrictive policies (Meier and McFarlane 1992, 695–696).

In a landmark study of the effects of abortion policy, Legge (1985, 129–131) found that a significant drop in abortion-related deaths occurred immediately after the *Roe v. Wade* ruling. However, when examining other indicators of maternal and infant health, no long-term significant changes were ushered in after the *Roe* ruling (Legge 1985, 130–140). Indeed, long-term reductions in infant mortality rates, neonatal mortality rates, and fetal death ratios were more closely tied to health and social spending increases enacted after 1967 and before the *Roe* decision (Legge 1985, 139).

Hansen (1980) found that the *Roe* decision had the effect of evening out the number of abortions across the states. In other words, the nationalization of abortion allowed states that did not provide abortion services to catch up with states that did. For example, in 1972, 84 percent of the abortions performed in the U.S. were in states that allowed for abortion on demand: New York, the District of Columbia, Alaska, Hawaii, and Washington. Four years later, only 35 percent of abortions were performed in those states (Hansen 1980, 381). An increasing number of abortions were being performed in states where abortion previously had been illegal.

Despite this trend toward geographic equalization of abortion rates, wide variations in abortion rates existed three years after the *Roe* ruling (Hansen 1980, 381–382). Abortion rates per 1,000 women aged 15–44 in 1976 varied from a high of 43 in New York to a low of 3 in West Virginia (Hansen 1980, 382). Wide disparities in the abortion rate continued to exist through the 1980s. In 1988, the highest and lowest abortion rates per women aged 15–44 could be found in California (49) and Wyoming (3) respectively (U.S. Centers for Disease Control and Prevention 1991, 24–25). Variation in abortion rates across the states has been attributed to different demographic bases: concentrations of urban centers, access to abortion providers, different policy restrictions, availability of Medicaid funds, and the presence of women in key legislative positions in state legislatures (Hansen 1980; Albritton and Wetstein 1991; Berkman and O'Connor 1992, 1993; Luttbeg 1992).

At the demographic level, several studies have found that states with high levels of personal income tend to have high numbers of abortion (Hansen 1980; Albritton and Wetstein 1991; Luttbeg 1992). A comparison of correlations between abortions per women aged 15–44 and demographic variables for the states in 1976 and 1992 are provided in table 12 (Hansen 1980; Albritton and Wetstein 1991; Luttbeg 1992, 354–359).

Several case studies of specific states have attempted to catalog the effects of policy changes in the abortion domain. For example, a Minnesota parental notification law that took effect in 1981 did lead to a decrease in pregnancies and abortion rates for women aged 15–17 (Rogers et al. 1991, 296). The parental notification law also had the effect of increasing the number of "late abortions" (after the 12th week of gestation) in the same age group (Rogers et al. 1991,

TABLE 12
Abortion Ratios - Pearson Correlation Coefficients

	1977	1980	1983	1988	1992
Percentage Metropolitan	.71	.67	.65	.61	.66
Per capita income	.40	.42	.42	.56	.71
Percentage Adults					
4 years college	.42	.39	.34	.32	.53
Pre-*Roe* abortion policy	.26	.22	.19	.25	.30
Percentage Women in					
State Legislature	.16	.12	.18	.10	.11

Sources: Hansen 1980; Albritton and Wetstein 1991; Luttbeg 1992

296). A study of a Massachusetts law turned up similar results. There, a 1981 law requiring parental or judicial consent resulted in a decrease in the number of abortions performed for minors in the state (Cartoof and Klerman 1986, 398). The Massachusetts law had the effect of increasing out-of-state abortions for women under age eighteen by 130 percent over the first four months of the new law (Cartoof and Klerman 1986, 398).

In a five-year study charting teenage abortions immediately after the *Roe* decision, scholars found that differences between blacks and other teens in abortion utilization began to narrow (Ezzard et al. 1982). While black teens tended to have more abortions than others, blacks also had higher levels of sexually active teens than other groups immediately after the 1973 Court ruling (Ezzard et al. 1982).

This review of the literature demonstrates that a wide variety of approaches have been used to examine the impact *Roe v. Wade* and policies in several states had on abortion rates. Researchers have roamed up and down the ladder of abstraction, focusing at different times on individual level data, state level data, and national aggregations. The statistical techniques have varied from time series analysis, pooled time series analysis, multiple regression, logistic regression, and case studies. Yet no one has used time series analysis to examine the influence *Roe v. Wade* had on abortion rates in the American states. The rest of this chapter provides such an analysis.

Data and Methods

Abortion rate data used in this study are derived from yearly summaries published by the U.S. Centers for Disease Control (CDC) and the National Center for Health Statistics. The data on abortions are reported from each state to the CDC on an annual basis. While the number of abortions reported to the CDC are slightly lower than statistics gathered by the Alan Guttmacher Institute

(Henshaw 1991), the correlation between the two sets of data is .95. National aggregate abortion rate data are available from the years 1966 to 1992.[1] Figure 1 is a graph of the raw time series for ratios of abortions to 1,000 live births over the 1966–1992 period. The variable essentially represents the proportion of abortions being obtained measured against births.

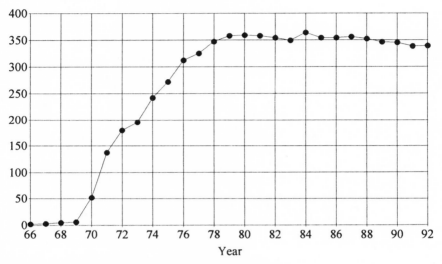

Figure 1. Ratio of Abortions to 1,000 Live Births, 1966–1992

A quick observation of figure 1 demonstrates two facts. First, the trend of an increasing abortion ratio was started prior to the 1973 *Roe v. Wade* decision and appears to follow the same trend line after the decision. Beginning in 1978, the abortion ratio starts to level off, apparently in conjunction with the prohibition of federal Medicaid funds for abortions.

Hypotheses

Four dummy variables are used to test different policy intervention hypotheses. The assumption behind these tests is that the impact of national policy changes (interventions) can be assessed using statistical methods. First, the *Roe v. Wade* intervention is modeled as a value of 0 prior to 1973 and a value

1. Data prior to 1969 are taken from surveys of abortion providers by the Alan Guttmacher Institute (Rosenberg 1991). Data for 1991 and 1992 are estimates calculated by the author based on a survey of abortion providers conducted by the Alan Guttmacher Institute in 1993 (Henshaw and Van Vort 1994, 104–112).

of 1 for each successive year. This implies that the abortion trend should have been affected in the years after the *Roe* decision. For the *Roe* decision to have a statistically significant effect on abortion rates, the estimate for this dummy variable must be significant. If not, we fail to reject the null hypothesis, that the *Roe v. Wade* decision had no impact on national abortion rates.

A second dummy variable tests the effect of the prohibition of federal Medicaid funds for abortions beginning in 1978 with the Hyde Amendment. Prior to 1978, yearly values for this variable were 0; 1978 and successive years had a value of 1 for this variable. Once again, if the estimate for this variable fails to be statistically significant, the null hypothesis cannot be rejected, and we cannot conclusively say that the withholding of federal Medicaid funds influenced national abortion rates.

A third variable models what some have called a "policy mood" that may have emerged on the abortion issue in the 1980s (Stimson 1991). This dummy variable codes years prior to the Reagan presidency as a 0 and years during the Reagan-Bush era as a 1. Such a treatment implies that the election of Republican presidents during the 1980s ushered in a conservative policy mood that may have dampened access to abortion. In a sense, this dummy variable serves as a surrogate measure for a host of converging forces, including Republican gains in the U.S. Senate, the appointment of an increasingly conservative federal and Supreme Court judiciary, and an increasingly vocal anti-choice lobby in the U.S. (Goggin and Wlezien 1993). If the Reagan-Bush variable fails to be significant, the null hypothesis of no impact on abortion rates cannot be rejected.

Finally, a dummy variable was created to assess the influence of the 1989 *Webster* decision on national abortion rates. In this case, years prior to 1989 are scored as a 0 and the 1989–1992 period is coded as 1. Once again, if the *Webster* variable fails to provide a significant estimate, the null hypothesis that *Webster* had no effect cannot be rejected.

The Interrupted Time Series Design

Two different levels of analysis are explored in this chapter. In the following section, national data are used to determine whether the *Roe* decision, the prohibition of Medicaid, the Reagan-Bush era, and the *Webster* ruling had statistically significant effects on national abortion rates. Next, several states are selected to test policy change hypotheses at the state level. This is done to determine if the national data mask patterns that can be discovered at the state level, a theoretically justified decision because we know from previous research that states vary widely in their abortion policies (Hansen 1980; Meier and McFarlane 1992, 1993; Goggin 1993; Segers and Byrnes 1995).

AutoRegressive Integrated Moving Average (ARIMA) modeling of the time series is the appropriate method to measure the impact of policy changes like the *Roe v. Wade* decision (Ostrom 1978; Cook and Campbell 1979; McDowall et al. 1980; McCleary and Hay 1980). The hypotheses take on the quality of a quasi-experimental design, suggesting that changes in the trend or series are a direct result of the specified event that takes place. While fifty observations is the standard rule of thumb in time series analysis, the smaller number of observations presented in this study do not preclude the use of time series analysis (Glass, Willson, and Gottman 1975, 200–202; Cook and Campbell 1979, 228–230; Judd and Kenny 1981). Shorter time series tend to make it more difficult to identify the appropriate ARIMA model to apply to the data, but the estimate of the intervention effect usually is reliable (Glass, Willson, and Gottman 1975, 200–202).

Because values for abortion rates are highly autoregressive, their error terms are likely to be correlated, which is a violation of a fundamental assumption of regression techniques. Thus, each successive observation and each successive error term is likely to be highly correlated. ARIMA modeling attempts to correct for this problem.[2] In the examples that follow, the ARIMA models were identified using a model building strategy outlined by Box and Jenkins (1976), and McDowall et al. (1980). The process included: (1) identification of a stationary time series with an appropriate autoregressive and moving average function, (2) ARIMA model estimates (p,d,q) that were significant and met criteria of stationarity and invertibility, and (3) diagnosis of time series residuals to ensure that the model had been reduced to a white noise process (McDowall et al. 1980, 47–54). Models reported in this study met the criteria for stationarity and invertibility, had significant parameter estimates for p or q, and had no significant Box-Ljung Q statistics.

---

2. The general ARIMA model is written as:

$$Y_t = N_t + I_t$$

in which N_t represents the time series reduced to a random white noise process, and I_t represents the intervention component. Three structural parameters are found in ARIMA models: p, an autoregressive parameter that represents the notion that Y_t is heavily determined by Y_{t-1}; d, a parameter that indicates the order of trend in the series or that each observation was subtracted from the previous observation in the series; and q, a parameter that models moving averages, or random shocks throughout the time series (McDowall, et al. 1980). An ARIMA (1,1,0) is a model that has been differenced once to reduce the series to a stationary process (d=1), with a first order autoregressive process (p=1), and no moving average component (q=0). ARIMA model identification attempts to reduce the trend or drift in a raw time series to a stationary white noise process, allowing for estimation of intervention variables.

National Findings

Table 13 presents the ARIMA time series estimates for the national abortion ratio series. Note that none of the policy variables have a statistically significant impact on abortion ratios. In short, the *Roe* decision (column 1), Medicaid (column 2), Reagan-Bush (column 3), and *Webster* (column 4) variables do not have a statistically significant impact on the trend in abortion rates. In fact, the *Roe* variable's estimate is in the unexpected direction (b = −19.54). This means that when controlling for the increasing trend already at work, and the apparent leveling off at an average around 1978, the *Roe* variable did not have a positive effect on the national abortion ratio. Two of the variables did have an impact in the expected direction: the Reagan-Bush variable (b = −9.23) and the *Webster* variable (b = −9.99). But because these estimates did not achieve statistical significance, we cannot conclusively argue that they had a negative influence on the abortion ratio.[3]

These findings from national data contradict popular claims about the impact of *Roe v. Wade*. Conventional wisdom tells us that *Roe* was the catalyst for a substantial increase in abortions in the United States. Yet time series analysis demonstrates that *Roe* did not significantly alter the trend in abortion utilization in this country, at least when examining aggregate data. Moreover, conventional wisdom that the federal Medicaid prohibition on abortion limited access to abortions in a significant way does not stand up to the test of time series analysis. Thus, advocates on both sides of the abortion debate might find something to quarrel with in this analysis. Advocates on both sides may disagree with the claim that *Roe v. Wade* did not matter in a statistical sense. Similarly, both camps might be troubled by the claim that the Hyde Amendment did not significantly alter national trends in abortion utilization.

The Impact of Roe: *A Different Dependent Variable.* To conclude that *Roe v. Wade* had no impact on abortions in this country would be misleading. Clearly it had the effect of legalizing first-trimester abortions in all fifty states. But the previous analysis indicates that the 1973 ruling did not significantly alter abortion rates in the United States. Perhaps this claim can be tempered somewhat with an analysis of a different dependent variable.

In the prior discussion, the dependent variable was the abortion rate in the United States. If the dependent variable were to be the percentage of out-of-state abortions obtained every year, a very different picture of *Roe*'s impact emerges

---

3. The time series equations were also estimated using a brief "pulse" effect for each of the four dummy variables. These models implied that the impact of the policy would last two years and then disappear. For example, the Roe variable was coded as a 1 in 1973 and 1974 only, and as a 0 for other years. Once again, all of these equations failed to establish significant effects from any of the variables.

TABLE 13
ARIMA Time Series Estimates—Ratio of Abortions to
1,000 Live Births, (1966-1992)

Independent Variables	1 b	2 b	3 b	4 b
Intercept	13.43*	11.94	13.04*	13.04*
	(5.95)	(6.01)	(5.91)	(5.83)
Roe v. Wade	−19.54	——	——	——
	(16.08)			
Federal Medicaid	——	19.84	——	——
		(15.85)		
Reagan-Bush	——	——	−9.23	——
			(17.04)	
Webster v. Reproductive Health Services	——	——	——	−9.99
				(17.27)
Moving Average	−.57*	−.59*	−.52*	−.51*
	(.15)	(.20)	(.18)	(.18)
Number of Cases	27	27	27	27
ARIMA Model	(0,1,1)	(0,1,1)	(0,1,1)	(0,1,1)

*p < .05 one-tailed test
standard errors are in parentheses

Roe v. Wade = 0 prior to 1973, 1 in 1973-1992 period
Federal Medicaid = 0 prior to 1978, 1 in 1978-1992 period
Reagan-Bush = 0 prior to 1981, 1 in 1981-1992 period
Webster v. Reproductive Health Services = 0 prior to 1989, 1 in 1989-1992 period

(U.S. Centers for Disease Control, various years).[4] Figure 2 presents a diagram of the percentage of abortions that were obtained by out-of-state residents from 1972 to 1989 (the years for which data are available). Note that in 1973 the percentage of out-of-state abortions drops dramatically, from 44 to 25 percent in one year. By 1974, the percentage of out-of-state abortions fell to about 12 percent, and hovered around 7 percent for most of the later years.

It is clear from figure 2 that *Roe v. Wade* did have a dramatic impact on where women obtained abortions. The legalization of abortion under *Roe* made it possible for many women to obtain abortions within their home states for the first time. While it is inappropriate to estimate the impact of *Roe* in this time series because there is only one pre-intervention measure, the impact of *Roe* on this dependent variable cannot be denied.

---

4. I am grateful to Jerome Legge for suggesting this operationalization of the dependent variable.

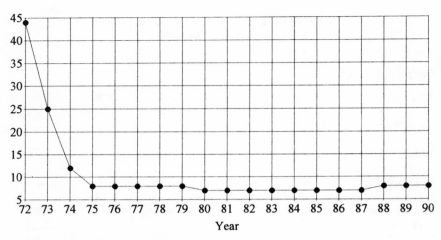

Figure 2. Percentage of Abortions Obtained Out of State

Measurement and Reporting of Abortions. The use of abortion data reported to the Centers for Disease Control may be inappropriate for measuring the true level of abortions nationally. In the years prior to *Roe*, only states that had legalized abortion were providing data to the federal government (U.S. Centers for Disease Control 1979). Thus, the data represent only reported legal abortions prior to 1973. The vast majority of unreported, illegal abortions are not included in the time series.

Therefore, the increase in abortions and abortion rates in the wake of *Roe* may represent better reporting of the real abortion rate. This might also explain the plateau of abortions and abortion rates around 1980. In essence, more systematic reporting of abortions by the states may have revealed the true abortion rate in the U.S. only around the 1979–1980 period. This also suggests that the supply and demand for abortions in this country settled into its equilibrium around that time as well.

Since dilation and curettage (D&C) is the most widely used method of performing abortions, it is instructive to compare abortion data with D&C data. By the late 1960s, obstetrics and gynecological specialists were familiar with the practice of performing D&C procedures (Gold et al. 1965; Schaefer 1971). Today, D&C is the most widely used method for performing abortions in the U.S. (Centers for Disease Control 1991). Indeed, more than 90 percent of all abortions for the last two decades have used this technique (Henshaw and Van Vort 1990).

Hospitals have been reporting the number of D&C surgical operations to the federal government during the same period that the Centers for Disease Control was collecting abortion data from the states (U.S. National Center for

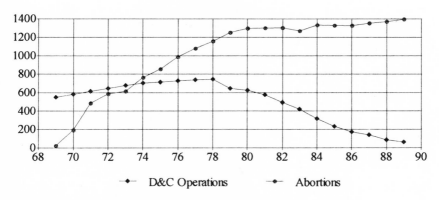

Figure 3. Legal Abortions and Hospital D&C Operations, 1969–1989

Health Statistics, various years). It must be emphasized that not all D&C operations are abortions, although nearly all abortions up to 1994 were D&C procedures. A graph of this data, therefore, indicates at least a portion of the abortions performed in hospitals over that period. When looking at aggregate numbers of abortions and D&C operations on women aged 15–44, a dramatic decline in hospital-reported D&C operations is noticeable beginning in the early 1980s (figure 3). Throughout the 1980s, D&C operations declined every year, to a low of about 60,000 in 1989.

This decline in hospital-reported D&Cs meshes well with the knowledge that more and more abortions were being performed in clinics and physician's offices during the 1980s (Henshaw 1991, Henshaw and Van Vort 1990; Tatalovich and Daynes 1989). Indeed, by 1988, more than 80 percent of all abortions in the U.S. were performed outside of hospitals. In short, the drop in hospital reporting of D&C operations may be an indicator of the changing nature of access to abortion in the United States.

It would be inappropriate to combine the two measures into an indicator of abortions in the American states. Hospital D&C operations that are abortions are undoubtedly included in the abortions reported to state health agencies and the Centers for Disease Control. In short, there may be contamination effects if researchers sought to combine the two variables as a measure of the true abortion rate. However, it is appropriate to test the impact of the federal Medicaid cutoff on the number of D&C operations obtained in U.S. hospitals. The hypothesis would be that the withdrawal of federal Medicaid funds for most abortions in 1978 led to a decline in D&C operations obtained in U.S. hospitals.

Table 14 is a representation of ARIMA time series estimates for the number of D&C operations obtained by women aged 15–44. The negative coefficient for the Medicaid variable indicates that withdrawal did have a negative impact on

TABLE 14
ARIMA Time Series Estimates—D&C Operations in U.S. Hospitals, 1969–1989

Independent variables	b
Intercept	23,263.1
	(50,742.6)
Federal Medicaid	−15,263.1
	(226,927.5)
Number of Cases	20
ARIMA Model	(0,1,0)

standard errors are in parentheses

Federal Medicaid = 0 prior to 1978, 1 in 1978–1989 period

D&C operations, although it is not statistically significant. The coefficient suggests that the Hyde Amendment led to a drop of 15,000 D&C operations.

State Findings

Medicaid in Colorado and Pennsylvania. The aggregation of data from fifty states might hide important changes in abortion rates in key states. With this in mind, a state level analysis might provide better insights into the true impacts of Medicaid and other policy changes. For instance, while federal Medicaid funds for abortions were largely eliminated under the 1978 Hyde Amendment, several state legislatures have attempted to continue abortion funding for the poor with their own state funding schemes. In 1992, twelve states had no restrictions on state Medicaid funded abortions, and five states (California, Connecticut, Massachusetts, New Jersey, and Vermont) did so only because of court orders invalidating restrictions on funding (NARAL 1992, 148).

Still, there are states where Medicaid policies for abortion have been in flux. For example, in 1984, Colorado introduced new restrictions on state funded abortions, limiting them only to cases of "life endangerment, fetal defect, or psychiatric conditions which might cause life endangerment" (Korenbrot et al. 1990, 557). The result of that new policy was a dramatic drop in Medicaid funded abortions in Colorado, with a decline from 1,610 cases in 1984 to only 10 in 1985 (Korenbrot et al. 1990, 557). Similarly, Pennsylvania legislators altered their Medicaid guidelines in 1985 to fund abortions only in cases of life endangerment, or when cases of rape or incest were reported to law enforcement officials (Korenbrot et al. 1990, 557). The result was a drop from more than 10,000 state funded abortions in 1984 to only 900 in 1985 (Korenbrot et al. 1990, 557; figures 4 and 5).

Time series analysis of Colorado and Pennsylvania abortion ratios demonstrate that new state prohibitions on Medicaid funded abortions did alter the

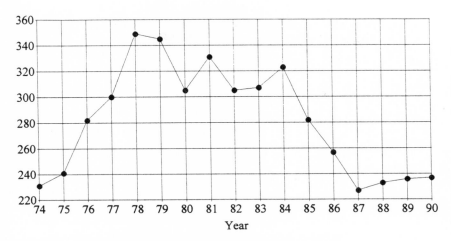

Figure 4. Colorado Abortion Ratio Per 1,000 Live Births, 1974–1990

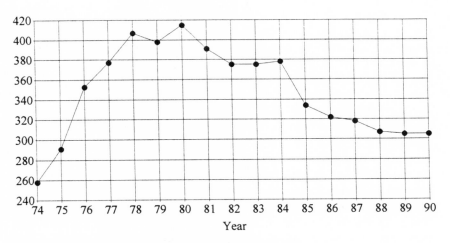

Figure 5. Pennsylvania Abortion Ratio Per 1,000 Live Births

number of abortions obtained. In Colorado, the ratio of abortions to 1,000 live births dropped from 323 in 1984 to 282 in the year after the prohibition. The decline in the abortion ratio in Pennsylvania was similar, falling from 378 to 334 between 1984 and 1985. Table 15 presents the ARIMA time series estimates for Colorado and Pennsylvania abortion ratios to 1,000 live births. The coefficients for the dummy variables modeling the change in state Medicaid funding have negative values, indicating that the number of abortions per 1,000 live births

TABLE 15
ARIMA Time Series Estimates
Abortion Ratio Per 1,000 Live Births, Colorado and Pennsylvania

Independent Variables	Colorado	Pennsylvania
Intercept	259.11**	5.70
	(17.34)	(10.32)
Federal Medicaid	54.91	22.79
	(19.32)	(17.62)
State Medicaid	−62.65**	−41.13**
	(18.28)	(17.62)
Autoregressive Function	.53**	.54**
	(.21)	(.23)
Number of Cases	17	17
ARIMA Model	(1,0,0)	(1,1,0)

**p < .05, *p < .1 one-tailed test
standard errors are in parentheses

Federal Medicaid = 0 prior to 1978, 1 in 1978–1990 period
State Medicaid = 0 prior to 1985, 1 in 1985–1990 period

dropped by 63 in Colorado and 41 in Pennsylvania after the change in policy. Both estimates for the impact of state Medicaid policy change are significant at the .05 level. This means that in Pennsylvania and Colorado, we can be 95 percent sure that the drop in the abortion ratio did significantly change after state Medicaid policy changes in 1985.

While caution should be used in drawing conclusions from such a short time series, the estimates do point in the expected direction: The negative and significant coefficient for the state Medicaid policy changes suggests that significant reductions occurred in the two states after state restrictions were enacted. These results run counter to national figures, which suggested that federal Medicaid restrictions had no impact on abortion ratio in the United States. The positive value for the federal Medicaid value in Colorado and Pennsylvania clearly means that the federal withdrawal of Medicaid funds did not have a dampening impact on abortion ratios in those states. Indeed, abortion ratios continued to rise.

State Policy Change: Parental Consent in Massachusetts. Massachusetts legislators enacted a parental consent law in 1981 that required unwed women under age 18 to obtain parental or judicial consent before having an abortion (Cartoof and Klerman 1986; Borreli 1995, 184). Previously, researchers have demonstrated that the law had a significant impact on the number of abortions obtained by women aged 17 and under in Massachusetts in the months following enactment of the law (Cartoof and Klerman 1986, 398–400). Indeed, the law had the effect of sending about 90 minors per month out of state to obtain abortions (Cartoof and Klerman 1986, 399).

Annual time series analysis suggests that the impact of the law can be seen well into the late 1980s. The ratio of abortions to 1,000 live births in Massachusetts declined from 605 in 1980 to 553 in 1981 (the year of enactment, figure 6). In 1982, the ratio was even lower (533), and was at 430 in 1989 and 1990. Table 16 presents time series estimates for Massachusetts abortion ratios per 1,000 live births.[5] The law led to a drop of 58 points in the ratio of abortions to 1,000 live births in Massachusetts the year after the law was implemented (across all age groups of women). The coefficient for parental consent is not significant, but it is in the expected direction.

State Policy Change: Court-Ordered Funding in California. In the wake of the federal government's effort to eliminate Medicaid funded abortions, California legislators also attempted to eliminate state Medicaid funds. Budget acts passed by the California legislature and signed into law in 1978, 1979, and 1980 excluded the use of state funds for elective abortions. Yet in 1981, the California supreme court declared the Medicaid restrictions unconstitutional (*Committee to Defend Reproductive Rights v. Myers*, Cal., 625 P.2d. 779; Russo 1995, 176).

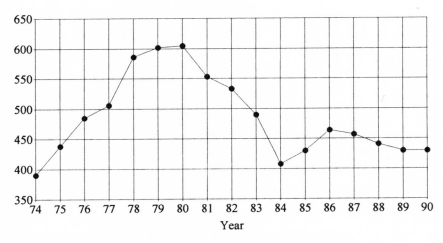

Figure 6. Massachusetts Abortion Ratio Per 1,000 Live Births, 1974–1990

5. The ideal measure to test the impact of the Massachusetts law would be the abortion ratio for women under the age of 18 across all years. Unfortunately, this data was not reported by Massachusetts to the U.S. Centers for Disease Control in early years.

TABLE 16
ARIMA Time Series Estimates
Massachusetts Abortion Ratio Per 1,000 Live Births, 1974–1990

Independent Variables	b
Intercept	435.02**
	(53.51)
Federal Medicaid	85.04
	(34.72)
Parental Consent	−57.68
	(34.28)
Autoregressive Function	.81**
	(.12)
Number of cases	17
ARIMA Model	(1,0,0)

** p < .05 one-tailed test
standard errors are in parentheses

Federal Medicaid = 0 prior to 1978, 1 in 1978–1990 period
Consent = 0 prior to 1981, 1 in 1981–1990 period

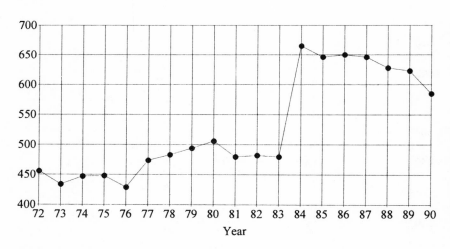

Figure 7. California Ratio of Abortions Per 1,000 Live Births, 1972–1990

The state was forced to provide state Medicaid money to poor women seeking abortions after that decision. Three years after the ruling was handed down, the abortion ratio per 1000 live births climbed from around 480 in 1981 to more than 640 in 1984 (figure 7). Since that time, abortion ratios to 1,000 live births have remained above or near 600 in California. Time series estimates

TABLE 17
ARIMA Time Series Estimates
California Abortion Ratio Per 1,000 Live Births, 1972–1990

Independent Variables	b
Intercept	–4.06
	(4.96)
Federal Medicaid	13.06
	(20.46)
State Medicaid	189.06**
	(20.46)
Number of cases	19
ARIMA Model	(0,1,0)

** p < .05
standard errors are in parentheses

Federal Medicaid = 0 prior to 1978, 1 in 1978–1990 period
Court Ruling = 0 prior to 1984, 1 in 1984–1990 period

indicate that the California court ruling resulted in a jump of 189 points in the abortion ratio in that state (table 17).[6] Moreover, the federal Medicaid withdrawal once again fails to demonstrate a negative effect on a state abortion ratio.

Conclusion

This study has used ARIMA time series models to demonstrate that the *Roe v. Wade* ruling and the prohibition of federal Medicaid funds for elective abortions failed to have a significant impact on abortion rates in this country. Yet analyses at the state level do demonstrate significant impacts of some state policy changes on abortion utilization.

Such a finding only reinforces the notion that state legislatures are the key to abortion policy in the United States. The devolution of abortion policy to the states is reflected in the current Supreme Court's tendency to allow states to regulate abortion as long as no "undue burden" is placed on women seeking abortions (*Webster v. Reproductive Health Services*; *Planned Parenthood of Southeastern Pennsylvania v. Casey*). Thus, with abortion policy increasingly in the domain of state legislatures and governors, it is not surprising that time series analysis should indicate that state policy change matters.

---

6. The California time series was modeled with a three year lag to allow for state budgeting of funds to the MediCal program.

Yet caution should be used in interpreting these results and applying them to all states. In this study, Massachusetts' parental consent law does not appear to have a significant impact on that state's abortion ratio. There may indeed be states in which policy change may not appear significant in a time series analysis. This study presents a few ideal states in which the impact of policy change is readily visible. Other states may not reflect the same patterns. More research needs to be done in this area to systematically characterize the impact of state policy changes on abortion utilization. This type of research will become more significant as states attempt to further restrict abortion access, and as more data points get added to the time series.

4

The Structure and Stability of Attitudes on Abortion

The customary approach to abortion attitude research is to regress abortion attitudes on an identified set of independent variables known to affect abortion views. For example, Granberg and Granberg (1980) used a set of demographic variables including education, income, age, race, sex, region, rurality, and occupational prestige to characterize support for abortion in the General Social Surveys of 1965, and 1972 through 1978. Their research suggested that respondents with higher socioeconomic backgrounds, nonsoutherners, and city dwellers were more likely to support abortion. The older the respondent, the less likely he or she was to support abortion in surveys.

In a single equation model, Granberg and Granberg (1980, 254) explained roughly 10 percent of the variance in the six-point abortion support scale of the General Social Survey. Combining these variables with indicators of conservatism toward matters of personal morality, they were able to boost their R Square values to around .25 (Granberg and Granberg 1980). Thus, the addition of questions on sexual permissiveness and teens having sex helped explain more of the support for abortion in the mass public. People who were less critical of sexual freedom tended to be less critical of abortion.

In the most sophisticated treatment of abortion attitudes to date, Cook, Jelen, and Wilcox (1992) have had the most success in accounting for the variance in abortion attitudes in the United States. Using a comprehensive collection of demographic, attitudinal, and religious variables, these researchers explained 38 percent of the variance in responses to six abortion questions in the General Social Surveys from 1987 to 1991 (Cook, Jelen, and Wilcox 1992, 123). The most significant variables in their analysis included age, education level, urbanization, general ideology, attitudes on sexual morality, euthanasia, and religious variables that tapped strength of conviction, denomination, and attitudes toward the Bible (Cook, Jelen, and Wilcox 1992, 121–124).

The attitudinal variables discussed by Cook, Jelen, and Wilcox (1992, 123) did not turn up any surprising findings. Respondents who opposed euthanasia were more likely to oppose abortion. Respondents who placed greater belief in the Bible were more likely to oppose abortion. Conservatives were much more likely to oppose abortion than liberals.

Much has also been written about the changing impact of variables on abortion attitudes. For example, the wide denominational differences that once existed between Catholics and mainline Protestants seem to have given way to a smaller gulf across denominational lines (Jelen 1988; Hertel and Hughes 1987; Gallup Report 1989; Gallup and Newport 1990). The gap between religious denominations is widest when comparing Protestant fundamentalist adherents with all other religions (Cook, Jelen, and Wilcox 1992). Jewish respondents are the most liberal on abortion, with 82 percent taking a consistent pro-choice stand over the 1972–1990 General Social Surveys (Cook, Jelen, and Wilcox 1992, 119–121).

Differences between blacks and whites on abortion have been disputed, with no apparent resolution (Baker, Epstein, and Forth 1981; Arney and Trescher 1976; Combs and Welch 1982; Hall and Feree 1986; Wilcox 1990, 1992 for differing opinions on the impact of race). Recent research by Clyde Wilcox (1992) suggests that the gap between blacks and non-blacks on abortion has narrowed, especially when controlling for religiosity and socioeconomic variables. Indeed, when controlling for religiosity and socioeconomic variables, recent surveys indicate that blacks are slightly more supportive of abortion than whites (Cook, Jelen, and Wilcox 1992, 44–48).

Legge (1983) used discriminant analysis to highlight the importance of religion and attitudes toward women's equality as predictors of abortion attitudes. Yet Legge found that only 44 percent of the cases could be classified correctly by his analysis, leading him to conclude that views on abortion were not structured strongly and not salient to the American public (Legge 1983, 488–489).

Legge's conclusion points to the apparent ambivalence most Americans have toward the abortion issue. Only a small portion of the American public occupy the pro-choice and anti-choice extremes. Roger Rosenblatt (1992, ch. 1) has maintained that abortion is one of the few issues Americans attempt to avoid in private conversation because of the nature of the dispute between the two extremes. Divisions between the two extremes have created a "muddled middle" that often casts a wary eye on public demonstrations by abortion supporters and opponents. Indeed, Goggin and Wlezien (1992) have maintained that interest group activities can push public attitudes on abortion in the opposite direction the group advocates.

Frauke Schnell (1993; 1991) has outlined the impact of a number of competing values on abortion attitudes. As Schnell and others have demonstrated, it is important to keep in mind that abortion attitudes are not formed in a vacuum separate from other attitudes. Clearly, issues like sexual liberalism, strength of religion, and attitudes about the role of the state in private affairs have the potential to conflict or interact with abortion attitudes (Schnell 1993; Cook, Jelen, and Wilcox 1992). Moreover, Schnell (1991) has pointed out that the strength of convictions on the abortion issue can have an impact on attitude stability.

What is needed now is a more sophisticated rendering of the relationships between abortion attitudes and the variables identified in previous research. Structural equation approaches to abortion attitudes have not been published in the political science literature. Quantitative methods beyond multiple regression have not been used with the data. This chapter presents a linear structural equation model (LISREL) model of abortion attitudes, offering a methodological update to the study of the structure of abortion attitudes.

A neglected problem in abortion attitude research is the consideration of attitude stability. Several scholars have attempted to pool data from a number of surveys, assuming that attitudes are relatively stable across time and therefore not significantly altered during the time between the sampling periods (Wright, Erikson, and McIver 1985, 1987; Erikson, Wright, and McIver 1993; Converse and Markus 1979). This concern with attitude stability must be addressed at both the aggregate level and the individual level if measures of abortion opinion for the states are to be created from different survey samples. A demonstration of attitude stability lends confidence to the process of pooling responses, while a demonstration of significant attitude instability would raise questions as to the utility of a pooled data approach.

Because abortion is an issue of incredible symbolic importance, and a potentially divisive issue (Goggin 1993), it is argued in this chapter that abortion attitudes should remain stable over time. The hypothesis behind such an approach is that when a controversial issue like abortion is in the public eye for a long period of time, attitudes become easy to form and difficult to change (Carmines and Stimson 1980). To paraphrase James Stimson (1991, 83), it is difficult to imagine an adult of childrearing age who has not thought about abortion as a public issue. American adults rarely select the "don't know" category when asked about abortion. Indeed, many Supreme Court watchers were incredulous when Justice Clarence Thomas, then a nominee, suggested at his confirmation hearings that he had "never personally engaged in discussions about abortion" (Craig and O'Brien 1993, 320).

The debate and rancor that surrounds the issue of abortion makes it relatively easy for individuals to form attitudes and remember their position on it. As Converse and Markus (1979, 42) put it, abortion is an issue

> Which pits the cutting edge of new mores against an array of traditional values...it is not entirely surprising that such moral issues should have a deeper resonance among those not normally attentive to much political controversy.

Because the abortion issue is so evident in public discourse, a central hypothesis of this chapter is that abortion attitudes are one of the most stable attitudes in the American public. Because the abortion issue is so controversial, attitudes on it are bound to be more stable than on other issues.

Measures of Aggregate Stability

Evidence for the aggregate stability of abortion opinions within the American public is abundant in the literature (Stimson 1991; Page and Shapiro 1992; Granberg and Granberg 1980; Ebaugh and Haney 1980; Gallup and Newport 1990; Glazer 1987; Legge 1983; Craig and O'Brien 1993). The years between 1965 and 1972 were marked by the apparent liberalization of opinions on abortion in the United States (Page and Shapiro 1992, 105–106; Rossi and Sitaraman, 1988; Craig and O'Brien 1993, 251). Since the *Roe v. Wade* decision in 1973, however, aggregate positions on abortion have remained stable.

The General Social Survey in almost every year since 1972 has asked respondents whether they support abortion for six reasons, ranging from abortion to protect the life of the pregnant woman to elective abortion. Over the years, there has been only a slight drop in the mean support level for the six reasons. For example, in 1972, the mean support stood at 3.9, indicating that on average, the American public supported four of the six reasons for abortion (Granberg and Granberg 1980, 253). Carrying this analysis forward into the 1980s, the stability of abortion support in the aggregate becomes clear. Table 18 provides the mean abortion support scores for the General Social Surveys in 1977, 1978, 1980, 1982, 1983, 1984, 1985, and 1987. The table also reports the percentage of the American public that supports each reason for an abortion, ranging from zero (no abortions at all) to six (allowing abortions for all circumstances).

The first set of figures in table 18 indicates that the mean level of support for abortion across the six questions has hovered between 3.5 and 4.0, with perhaps a slight decline in the mean level of support over the period. The bottom set of figures indicates the percentage of respondents supporting abortion for a specific number of reasons. The data demonstrate there is a core group of about 10 percent within the American public that would prohibit abortion for any reason. During the 1977–1987 period, roughly a third of the American public supported the right to an abortion for all six circumstances. In between these two extremes are the majority of Americans, about 60 percent, who have differing views about the legal circumstances for abortion.

What is important about table 18 is the relative stability in the cell percentages across the number of years. The greatest gap for any change between the two endpoints in the period is four percentage points. Between 1977 and 1987 there was a four-point increase in absolute opposition to abortion and a four-point decline in absolute support for abortion. While some would contend this is evidence of remarkable stability, given the error-prone nature of public opinion measurement, others would point to the changes and make different arguments. For example, Goggin and Wlezien (1993) argue that there were significant changes in attitudes on abortion in the 1988–1989 period just prior to the *Webster* ruling by the Supreme Court. They contend that public opinion on

TABLE 18
Approval of Abortion Circumstances in General Social Surveys, 1977–1987

	77	78	80	Year of Survey 82	83	84	85	87
Mean	3.95	3.73	3.89	3.79	3.53	3.69	3.62	3.55
Percentage Supporting								
0 Reasons	8	9	9	10	11	9	10	12
1	6	6	6	5	8	8	8	7
2	9	10	10	10	12	11	12	11
3	21	24	21	23	22	23	23	23
4	11	12	10	10	10	8	9	9
5	11	9	9	9	8	6	7	7
6 Reasons	35	30	37	34	29	35	32	31

Compiled from General Social Surveys, 1977–1987

abortion was merely responding to the increased interest group competition and court activity in the abortion arena (Goggin and Wlezien 1993).

Scholars have argued that any slight shift in aggregate opinion deserves some fanfare, especially when attitudes have appeared to be stable in the past (Stimson, 1991, ch. 1). Yet it would be unwise to attribute any significance to the decline of a few points in the support score. It may be attributable to changes in the order of questions in the General Social Survey over the years (Rossi and Sitaraman, 1988; Bishop, Oldendick, and Tuchfarber 1985). In short, the change in abortion support may be an artifact of the survey and question context, and not based in some inherent change in attitudes within the public. Thus, imprecise measurement might account for any slight declines in the abortion responses.

Recent data from the General Social Survey suggest that aggregate public opinion on abortion has not dramatically changed since the *Webster* ruling in 1989 (Craig and O'Brien 1993, 254; Cook, Jelen, and Wilcox 1992, 37–38). Table 19 provides a listing of responses to abortion questions on the General Social Survey for several years between 1978 and 1991. Note that between 1989 and 1991, there are slight increases of support for the "hard" reasons for obtaining an abortion, such as when a woman's health is in danger and rape. On the whole, however, there is no significant movement in abortion opinions across the set of questions (for a contrary argument, see Goggin and Wlezien 1993).

Another way to assess stability of abortion attitudes at the aggregate level is to track attitudes within a state over time. Fortunately, the Illinois Policy Survey has asked a series of repeated questions on the abortion issue in the years 1990 through 1992 (Center for Governmental Studies 1990, 1991, 1992). Responses to the question over the three-year period are presented in table 20. It is clear from the table that a consistent 37 to 40 percent of Illinoisans favor abortion as a legal option in all cases. This display of stability across three different samples

TABLE 19

Abortion Opinion Results from the General Social Survey, 1974–1991

Question: Please tell me whether or not you think it should be possible for a pregnant woman to obtain a legal abortion.

Percent Saying Yes
Year

	1978	1980	1982	1984	1987	1989	1990	1991
if the woman's health is seriously endangered	90	90	92	90	89	94	92	92
if she became pregnant as a result of rape	84	83	86	80	81	89	85	86
if there is a strong chance of serious defect in the baby	86	83	84	80	79	81	81	83
if the family has a low income and cannot afford any more children	47	52	52	46	45	46	48	48
if she is not married and does not want to marry the man	41	48	49	44	42	44	45	45
if she is married and does not want any more children	40	47	48	43	42	40	45	45

Sources: National Opinion Research Center, General Social Surveys, 1978–1991, survey results reported in Public Opinion, *May/June 1989, 37; and Craig and O'Brien 1993, 252–254.*

TABLE 20

The Stability of Abortion Attitudes in the Illinois Policy Survey

Question: Regardless of how you personally feel about abortion, do you think it should be legal in all cases, legal in some cases, or not legal in any case?

| | Year of Survey | | |
	1990	1991	1992
Legal in all cases	38%	37%	39%
Legal in some cases	45	49	45
Not legal	14	11	13
Won't answer	2	3	3
Sample Size	831	800	801

Source: Center for Governmental Studies, Illinois Policy Survey Codebooks, 1990, 1991, 1992

and three different years after the *Webster* ruling is one more piece of evidence supporting the claim that aggregate attitudes on abortion are stable.

A word of caution is in order. The relationships mentioned so far have focused on aggregated data at different points in time. The relationships do not follow an individual over time. In other words, while the data present several snapshots over time, the data do not present the same people in those snapshots. The most promising way to examine this issue is to use panel data from the American National Election Studies to catalog attitude stability over time at the individual level.

Measures of Individual Stability

The question of attitude stability has troubled the discipline since the early 1960s. One of the opening claims of instability was brought by Philip E. Converse (1964) in his now-famous article "The Nature of Belief Systems in Mass Publics." In a three-pronged argument, Converse found no constraint or consistency in political attitudes within the American public. First, he argued that only a small minority (about 2 to 4 percent) could be labeled ideologically sophisticated (Converse 1964, 214–219). Second, he found little systematic continuity between issue areas, indicating that political attitudes often appeared to be set off in separate belief systems rather than in one organized system (Converse 1964, 229). Finally, Converse (1964, 239–245) used panel study data to demonstrate that there is little correlation over time on specific issue positions within the mass public (except for party affiliation). That is, Americans had a strong tendency to respond differently in different years, indicating unstable attitude positions on political issues.

Since that time, Converse has withstood criticism and garnered support within the discipline. Nie, Verba, and Petrocik (1979), relying on data from the

1960s and 1970s, argued that the American electorate became more ideo-logically sophisticated during those trying political times. Unfortunately, their results were based on question formats that had been altered, biasing the data in their favor (Kinder 1983, 395). Indeed, controlling for the question changes, other researchers found the electorate to be just as ideologically unsophisticated in the 1960s as in the 1950s (Kinder 1983; Smith 1989).

Even symbolic issues like attitudes toward race relations were found to be unstable over time in early panel studies. Converse (1964) found only a .48 correlation over the 1958–1960 panel on a question dealing with the govern-ment's role in desegregating schools. Recently, Smith (1989) has argued that low levels of attitude stability and constraint in the American electorate have gone unchanged: The American voter is as ideologically unsophisticated and unstable as the voter Converse described. Party identification still remains relatively stable, but specific issue correlations across time fell well below the stability of party identification.

Yet there are increasing claims to the contrary arguing for stable attitudes in the American electorate. Morris Fiorina's (1981) model of retrospective voting implies that party affiliation is as subject to change as other attitudes. Thus, party identification is potentially as stable (or unstable) as other attitudes. More recently, Krosnick (1991, 561) reexamined NES panel data (using LISREL to estimate stability coefficients) and found equal levels of stability for party identification, ideological orientations, racial issues, nonracial policy issues, and matters of political efficacy and trust. In other words, party identification's supreme role in the attitude stability debate may no longer be appropriate.

Two possible findings could emerge in an analysis of abortion attitudes in panel studies. Under the Converse scenario, abortion attitudes will be much less stable than party identification. Krosnick's recent findings contradict this claim, implying that abortion attitudes can be as stable as party identification.

For this study, the stability of abortion attitudes was tested using the 1972–1976 National Election Panel Study. Comparisons were made between party identification across the four-year span, as well as responses to an abortion question that was asked in both years.[1] The test is to determine how closely

---

1. The question wording was:

"There has been some discussion about abortion in recent years. Which one of the opinions on this card best agrees with your view? You can just tell me the number of the opinion you choose:

1. abortion should never be permitted.
2. abortion should be permitted only if the life and health of the woman is in danger.
3. abortion should be permitted if, due to personal reasons, the woman would have difficulty in caring for the child.
4. abortion should never be forbidden, since one should not require a woman to have a child she doesn't want."

abortion attitudes match across the four-year time frame and compare them to party identification correlations (Converse and Markus 1979). Note that this four-year gap represents a stringent test of the stability hypothesis for two reasons. First, four years is a significant span of time to test issue agreement for an individual. Second, the *Roe v. Wade* decision falls between the two survey periods. This was clearly an era of intense abortion debate, and if there were ever to be switching of attitude positions because of education on the issue, the 1972–1974 period stands out as the benchmark to examine.

Examining correlation coefficients, we see a verification of the claims by Krosnick (1991). The Pearson correlation coefficient for party identification across the two surveys is .68. The correlation coefficient for the abortion question in 1972 and 1976 is .62. Thus, the stability of the abortion question over time rivals the stability of party identification in the 1972–1976 panel study. The results are similar to party identification correlations reported by Converse (1964) in the 1958–1960 panel study (.74), and the average correlation (.60) across a number of subgroups reported in the 1972–1976 panel study by Krosnick (1991).

Further analysis of attitude positions on abortion in the 1972–1976 panel study points even more directly to the stability of abortion attitudes at the individual level. Sixty percent of the individuals in the NES panel gave the same attitude response in 1976 that they gave in 1972. Moreover, if the definition of stability is relaxed to allow individuals to move one issue position on the abortion scale, 90 percent of the individuals in the panel study could be said to have stable abortion attitudes.

The evidence presented in this chapter may add to the growing debate surrounding attitude stability. The divisive nature of the abortion issue and its long tenure on the public agenda have helped to solidify individual attitudes on abortion. Attitudes on abortion appear to be less vulnerable to change than other issues, and apparently as stable as party identification. Moreover, aggregate patterns of abortion attitudes have remained remarkably stable over the past fifteen years. Such findings lend confidence to the practice of pooling abortion data from different surveys. The next chapter presents public opinion data for each of the fifty states using such a method. Before turning to that issue, a linear structural equation model of abortion attitudes is presented as a methodological update to the study of abortion attitudes.

A LISREL Model of Abortion Attitudes

This section characterizes American public opinion on abortion in 1988 and 1989, as recorded in the General Social Survey. The dependent variable consists of responses to abortion circumstances in cases of danger to the woman's health, rape or incest, birth defects, a woman not wanting to marry, a poor woman who cannot afford another child, and a married woman who does not want any more children. In a structural equation model, these six attitudes were modeled as tapping one latent construct that shapes abortion attitude responses.[2]

The independent variables explaining abortion attitudes are a core set of demographic and attitudinal variables that have often been used in abortion research. They include: whether a respondent opposed premarital sex; whether a respondent opposed teens having sex; frequency of church attendance; a measure of religious intensity based on self-reported strength of religious affiliation; the expanded coding of city size; the age of the respondent; the highest level of education completed by the respondent; and an occupational prestige score.[3]

Hypotheses

Based on prior research, it was expected that respondents with more liberal views on premarital sex and teens having sex would tend to have more liberal views on the six abortion questions (Granberg and Granberg 1980; Cook, Jelen, and Wilcox 1992). In contrast, more religious respondents, with greater frequencies of church attendance, were expected to be less favorable to abortion under the six circumstances. Older respondents also were expected to have more conservative views on abortion. Respondents with lower levels of education and occupational prestige were hypothesized to be less favorable to abortion than their better educated and better paid counterparts (Granberg and Granberg 1980; Mileti and Barnett 1972; Cook, Jelen, and Wilcox 1992).

City size has been infrequently used in models of abortion opinion, despite an apparent connection (Granberg and Granberg 1980; Mileti and Barnett 1972; Cook, Jelen, and Wilcox 1992). In previous research, it has been easy to see the aggregate connection between city size and abortion utilization (Hansen 1980; Powell-Griner and Trent 1987; Tatalovich and Daynes 1989). Large cities have more abortion providers, making an urban/rural cultural cleavage important for abortion utilization research. Such a cleavage might shape abortion attitudes as well. The hypothesis is that large metropolitan areas may induce more liberal approaches to abortion.

---

2. An alternate model would have included two separate abortion factors: one dealing with the so-called "hard" abortion questions (rape, birth defect, and health reasons) and one centering on the so-called "soft" abortion questions (no more children, single woman, and poor woman). Such a specification was impossible because of identification problems (Asher 1983).

3. The General Social Survey cases were weighted to correct the sample for the number of adults in each household, as suggested in the cumulative codebook provided by the National Opinion Research Center (Davis and Smith 1990).

Methods

The independent variables described were used in a principal components analysis to identify underlying factors that might shape abortion attitudes.[4] Results of the analysis are reported in table 21. The first factor seems to tap attitudes on religiosity and moralism. Attitudes on strength of religious intensity (.872) and church attendance (.873) load very strongly on this factor. Attitudes on premarital sex load moderately on this factor as well (.416). A second factor taps attitudes on sexual liberalism, with premarital sex (.640), teen sex (.730),

TABLE 21
Factor Loadings on Six Abortion Questions on General Social Surveys, 1988–1989

Factor

Variable	Religious/ Moral	Sexual Liberalism	Socioecon. Status	City Size
Church Attendance	.873			
Religious Intensity	.872			
Premarital Sex	.416	.640		
Teen Sex		.730		
Age		−.747		
Education			.847	
Occupational Prestige			.897	
City Size				.975

Note: Factor loadings under .3 are omitted from this table.

---

4. A single multiple regression equation was also tested to replicate prior research. The six-point abortion scale served as the dependent variable. Variables were recoded to have the highest value represent the most liberal or most supportive abortion position. The equation explained 31 percent of the variance in the scale (R square = .307). All of the variables were significant at p = .05 or better. Unstandardized coefficients, standardized coefficients, and T values for the variables are as follows:

Variable	b	T	Beta
Premarital Sex	.515	11.4	.32
Education	.130	7.1	.20
Age	.017	5.7	.14
City Size	.095	5.7	.13
Religious Intensity	.259	4.6	.13
Church Attendance	.086	3.8	.11
Occupational Prestige	.010	2.6	.07
Teen Sex	.161	2.6	.06
Constant	−1.487	−4.0	

and age (–.747) all loading strongly. The third factor is a socioeconomic factor, with high loadings for education level (.847) and occupational prestige (.897). City size returned the only large loading on a fourth factor (.975).[5]

Using the principal components analysis results as a guide, a LISREL structural equation model was developed to characterize the relationships between the abortion attitudes and the other variables. The four factors (religious/moral, sexual liberalism, socioeconomic, and urban/rural) suggested causal paths that would influence a latent abortion attitudes factor. This abortion factor would influence the various attitudes respondents have on the six abortion questions in the General Social Survey.

In the hypothesized LISREL model, age is designated as an exogenous variable that affects the underlying factor for sexual liberalism. This underlying factor on sexual permissiveness serves as the driving force for the two endogenous variables dealing with sexuality (teen sex and premarital sex). The urban/rural factor is an unobserved factor that hypothetically drives respondent answers on city size. It is hypothesized that this urban/rural factor influences the sexual liberalism of a respondent, as well as attitudes on abortion. Similarly, the socioeconomic factor is unmeasured but influences two observed endogenous variables: education and occupation prestige. This socioeconomic factor may affect the sexual liberalism and abortion attitudes factors. Finally, the religious/moral factor is hypothesized as having an impact on sexual liberalism and abortion attitudes. The religious factor is tied to two measured endogenous variables of church attendance and religiosity. A diagram of the hypothesized LISREL model is provided in figure 8.

The estimated model allows for correlation of the error terms between the three hard abortion questions and the three soft questions. Additionally, a small amount of error was estimated for the age and city size paths.[6] Simultaneous estimation of the equations indicates that the hypothesized model fits the data rather well. The low Chi Square value of 185.2 for 65 degrees of freedom is a good indication that the model is reproducing the covariance matrix (Long 1983a, 65; Long 1983b). The ratio of Chi Square to degrees of freedom is 2.8, below the standard of 3.0 that serves as a rule of thumb for model fitting (Long 1983b; Joreskog and Sorbom 1986). The Goodness of Fit Index is .971, nearly

---

5. Only the first two factors had Eigen values in excess of 1.0. A four-factor solution was predetermined on theoretical grounds, based on an examination of the questions and previous research. The four factors explain 74 percent of the variance.

6 The value for the age theta delta was set at one percent error, under the assumption that there would be very little measurement error in reported age. The value for the city size theta epsilon was set at ten percent error, under the assumption there would be slightly higher levels of error in reporting of size of city.

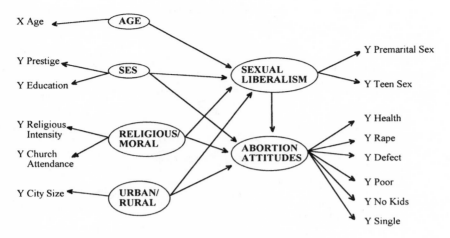

Figure 8. A Hypothesized LISREL Model of Abortion Attitudes

approaching the desired level of 1.0. These values inspire confidence that the specified model fits the data well. (Asher 1983; Joreskog and Sorbom 1986).

Figure 9 provides the LISREL estimates for the measurement model. The religious/moral factor has the greatest influence on the abortion attitude factor (Beta = .32). Next in importance are the socioeconomic factor (Beta = .30) and the sexual liberalism factor (.29), with the urban/rural factor having the smallest impact (.19). Moreover, the religious/moral factor plays an important role in shaping attitudes on sexual liberalism (Beta = .43). Socioeconomic status (Beta =.21) and age (Gamma = −.21) also have significant impacts on the sexual liberalism factor.

The path coefficients indicate that all four of the hypothesized factors play some role in shaping the structure of abortion attitudes. Individuals with more liberal views on premarital and teen sex tend to have more liberal views on abortion. Respondents with little or no ties to strong religious practices tend to support abortion under more circumstances than strongly religious respondents. Higher socioeconomic respondents tend to have more liberal abortion attitudes. Residents of larger metropolitan areas also tend to be more supportive of abortion under various circumstances. Note that the minus sign for the path between age and sexual liberalism indicates that older respondents tend to be more conservative on issues of sexual liberalism.

The effect of the correlation among the six abortion questions can be seen in table 22. There are moderate loadings from each of the error terms to the abortion questions, as well as low correlations between the error terms for the questions.

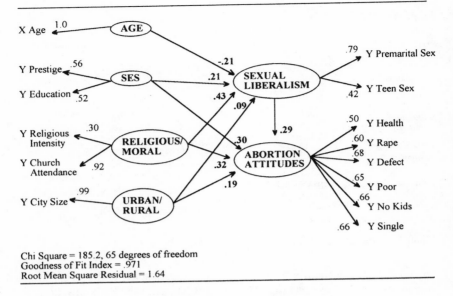

Chi Square = 185.2, 65 degrees of freedom
Goodness of Fit Index = .971
Root Mean Square Residual = 1.64

Figure 9. Estimates for a LISREL Model of Abortion Attitudes

TABLE 22
Correlation of Error Terms in the LISREL Model

	Defect	Rape		Poor	Single
Health	.248	.265	No More Kids	.333	.368
Defect		.187	Poor		.330

Note: Values are theta epsilon estimates for the abortion question error terms not shown in figure 9.

Overall, the factors and variables in the LISREL model explain 43 percent of the variance in the abortion attitude factor, with 57 percent of the variance remaining unexplained. Moreover, simultaneous estimation allows us to see that 29 percent of the variance in the sexual liberalism factor is accounted for in the model.

The LISREL model produces higher levels of explanation found in previous multiple regression equation models. For example, Granberg and Granberg (1980) used fourteen variables to explain 32 percent of the variance in the abortion support scale in the 1977 General Social Survey. Cook, Jelen, and Wilcox (1992) used 18 variables to explain 38 percent of the variance in the abortion support scale in the 1987–1991 General Social Surveys. The LISREL model presented in this chapter produces an R Square value of .43 with only four latent factors and a total of eight observed indicators.

Conclusion

Several conclusions emerge from the foregoing analysis of abortion attitudes. The stability and structure of abortion attitudes outlined in this chapter suggest that policymakers will face a relatively predictable mass public on the abortion issue in the next few years. Americans have come to hold stable views on abortion, and the ideological polarization of the issue is likely to continue under a new presidential administration.

This chapter suggests that relatively stable attitudes on abortion were evident during the four years (1972–1976) when abortion policy was in transformation in this country. It is remarkable that abortion attitudes remained so constant at the individual level during the era when *Roe v. Wade* was decided. Such a finding implies that attitudes in the mass public are unlikely to be greatly swayed by recent or forthcoming court decisions. Some scholars may debate this issue (Goggin and Wlezien 1991, 1993), but the *Webster* decision by the Supreme Court in 1989 and recent decisions like *Casey v. Reproductive Health Services* (1992) are unlikely to have a marked impact on abortion attitudes. The arguments in this chapter suggest that individuals in the U.S. have examined the abortion issue and plan largely to retain the beliefs they have, despite changes in the political environment.

This is not to say, however, that interest groups will not attempt to sway abortion attitudes. As Goggin (1993) has argued, interest groups on both sides of the abortion dispute have used court decision shocks to either alter their tactics or attempt to expand the scope of conflict by drawing in new supporters. Ostensibly, these supporters come from the ambivalent muddled middle in the mass public. The 1989 *Webster* ruling by the Supreme Court served as a catalyst for pro-choice activists to draw long-dormant pro-choice supporters into the streets for symbolic marches. Yet these shocks and changes in the abortion landscape have occurred periodically since 1973, and remarkably, attitudes on abortion have shown little movement.

The stability of abortion attitudes in the American public has important implications for policymakers. Such stability allows legislators and policymakers the luxury of working in a political environment that features relatively predictable mass opinions. For example, Illinois legislators need only turn to Illinois Policy Survey results to learn that Illinoisans are unlikely to radically alter their views on the abortion issue. Thus, state legislators can be comforted by the notion that public opinion on abortion is likely to remain stable over the next few years. While that opinion often appears to be divisive and confrontational at the extremes, policymakers at least can be assured of stable attitudes in the mass public.

The agenda of abortion liberalization that has emerged under the Clinton administration will serve to fuel the battles between pro-choice and pro-life advocates. Just as *Webster* and *Casey* have boosted membership and activities in abortion rights interest groups, legislative moves in 1993 and 1994 by a Democratic Congress and the Clinton administration mobilized pro-life support. Clinton's decision to overturn a number of executive orders by the Reagan and Bush administrations shifted the fortunes of abortion interest groups, and could have a dramatic impact on state abortion policies. For example, the Clinton administration's policy requiring states to use Medicaid funds for abortions when women are victims of rape and incest has brought legal challenges from several states. Thus, the scope and nature of the national abortion conflict, which certainly changed in the wake of the *Webster* ruling (Goggin 1993) and the 1992 presidential election, is certain to change again in the wake of the 1994 congressional elections and the 1996 elections. The findings in this chapter suggest that the bulk of the mass public, however, will remain outside that conflict.

Finally, the demonstration that abortion attitudes are stable at the individual and aggregate level allows researchers to pool responses from surveys into one data set. As long as question wordings are similar (if not identical), we can be confident that responses given in 1993 will be similar (if not identical) to responses given in 1992. Such a finding allows us to construct state opinion scores for the first time on abortion questions. Chapter 5 explores the variation in abortion attitudes in the fifty states, and correlates the mean score of abortion attitudes with abortion policy and abortion rates.

5

State Public Opinion and Abortion Policy

The impact of public opinion on abortion policy in the states has received little attention in the political science literature (see Goggin and Wlezien 1993 for an exception). Indeed, the seminal study on abortion utilization by Hansen (1980) omitted state public opinion from the list of explanatory variables because of the unavailability of public opinion data at the state level. Omitting opinion on abortion from any causal model that seeks to explain state abortion policy seems questionable, given our knowledge of the wide variation in state policies and the wide variation in support for abortion by mass publics across the states. For example, where survey data is available, it is easy to see a strong correlation between public opinion and abortion policy. A 1989 survey of Illinoisans found that 46 percent of the public wanted abortion laws to be "kept the way they are" (Center for Governmental Studies 1989). Yet in a 1989 CBS News/*New York Times* survey, 63 percent of Californians surveyed wanted abortion laws to be kept the same. Not surprisingly, abortion laws in California are significantly more liberal than in Illinois, with California providing state Medicaid money for all types of abortions.

Mixed results on public opinion's connection to abortion policy have been reported elsewhere. Johnson and Bond (1982) found little responsiveness by local hospital administrators to local pressure groups on the abortion issue. Although interest groups seem to have little impact, a large portion of hospital administrators (79 percent) reported that their abortion policies were "consistent with community preferences" (Johnson and Bond 1982). Their research implies that abortion policies in hospitals were in line with public opinion on abortion.

Until recently there have been a number of problems with collecting state public opinion data. First, there was the problem of availability of data. Until recently, there was no source of consistent data available to researchers at the state level for all fifty states on the issue of abortion. Indeed, a collection of state polls at the National Network of State Polls at the University of North Carolina turned up only thirteen state surveys with abortion questions (Dran, personal communication 1993). Wright, Erikson, and McIver (1987; Erikson, Wright, and McIver 1993) were able to get around this difficult problem by pooling a number of random sample national polls over a decade to obtain measures of the liberalism of the states. Their analysis benefited from a standardized question about a person's ideology asked in virtually every poll. Until recently, such an approach was not available in the abortion area, because polling organizations have only recently begun to repeat the same question. Thus, any attempt at including abortion public opinion in a causal analysis had to rely on surrogate measures, such as congressional voting on abortion (Hansen 1980). Other researchers have attempted to create instrumental variables that they believe reflect the opinion distribution of the states (Weber and Shaffer 1972; Weber et al. 1972).

It is only recently that reliable state public opinion data has become available to researchers. In 1990, exit polls were taken in forty-two of the fifty states, including an abortion question (CBS News/*New York Times* 1991). With such a wide distribution of states covered, and random sampling frames, political scientists are just beginning to turn to this source of data (Goggin and Wlezien 1991, 1993). Yet states that are significant for abortion policy study are missing from the 1990 exit polls, including Louisiana and Utah (Norrander and Wilcox 1993).

In light of this failing (albeit a small one compared to earlier methods), some scholars have turned to an emerging source of data in the National Election Series Senate Panel Studies for the years 1988, 1990, and 1992 (Norrander and Wilcox 1993). The benefit of this data set is its comprehensive coverage of all fifty states, with sample sizes approaching or exceeding 100 for each state.

Norrander and Wilcox (1993) pooled data from the first two waves of these surveys and found high correlations between the data and the 1990 CBS/*New York Times* exit polls. Such findings inspire confidence in the NES panel data. Despite smaller sample sizes, which tend to inflate errors in the data, the NES data match up well with other survey data.

This chapter outlines the variation in state public opinion on abortion issues. The focus is on the aggregate level of support for keeping abortion legal, support for government funded abortions, and opposition to parental consent provisions within each state. Demographic variables are used to explain the differences in state public opinion on abortion. In the final section of the chapter, public opinion measures are correlated with abortion policy and abortion rates in the fifty states to demonstrate the impacts public opinion can have on abortion utilization.

State Public Opinion on Abortion Issues

The 1988 and 1990 National Election Series Senate Panel Study contains several questions on abortion. The wording of the abortion questions follows:

Do you think abortions should be legal under all circumstances, only legal under certain circumstances, or never legal under any circumstance?

Would you favor or oppose a law in your state that would allow the use of government funds to help pay for the costs of abortion for women who cannot afford them?

Would you favor or oppose a state law that would require parental consent before a teenager under 18 could have an abortion.

The questions touch on three of the major themes in the abortion dispute over the past two decades. The first question essentially gauges public support for *Roe v. Wade* and a woman's right to an abortion. The second question measures support for public funding of abortions when a woman cannot afford them, which was essentially eliminated at the federal level by the Hyde Amendment in the late 1970s. The third question deals with parental consent provisions that have been enacted by most states.

Table 23 lists the mean level of support found within each state on each of the questions. The states are listed in their order of support for abortion being legal in all circumstances. The lowest amount of support is found in Kentucky (12 percent), and the highest amount of support for abortion is in Colorado (48 percent). On average, nearly a third of the states' populace favors a woman's right to abortion under any circumstance.

Generally, southern states have the lowest levels of public support for abortion. Of the ten least pro-choice states, seven could be classified as southern or border states (Kentucky, West Virginia, Mississippi, Arkansas, Missouri, Louisiana, and Georgia). Students familiar with Daniel Elazar's typology of political culture in the states would not be surprised to find that traditionalist states are among the most conservative states on abortion issues (Elazar 1984). The most supportive mass publics tend to represent northeastern and Pacific coast states.

The fourth column in table 23 provides the ratio of abortions to 1,000 live births in 1992 as a yardstick to measure the relationship between public opinion and utilization of abortion. Note that in states where support for abortion under all circumstances is high, abortion rates tend to be highest. For example, New York has the highest abortion ratio of all fifty states (694 for every 1,000 live births). It also features a very pro-choice populace, with 40 percent of the NES respondents supporting abortion under any circumstance. New Yorkers also gave the strongest support to government funding of abortions (70 percent), and more than a third (38 percent) oppose parental consent provisions. Similarly, Hawaii has the second highest abortion ratio (617), and a very pro-choice public. In contrast, states with low support for abortion in the mass public tend to have lower abortion rates. For example, West Virginia has one of the lowest levels of support for abortion in the mass public (only 13 percent favor abortion under any circumstance). The state also has one of the lowest ratios of abortion to live births (134 per 1,000 live births). Kentucky presents a similar picture, with low

TABLE 23
State Public Opinion on Abortion Issues, 1988–90 NES Surveys

State	Percent Favoring Abortion All Cases	Percent Who Favor Government Funding	Percent Who Oppose Parental Consent	Ratio of Abortions to 1,000 Births, 1992
Kentucky	12	29	33	191
W. Virginia	13	38	21	134
Mississippi	15	42	39	176
Arkansas	16	43	14	213
Missouri	19	35	29	175
N. Dakota	20	44	26	149
Louisiana	20	32	25	195
Wisconsin	22	41	20	223
Utah	22	37	17	104
Georgia	23	28	22	350
Kansas	23	42	22	353
Tennessee	23	37	28	243
S. Dakota	24	29	20	92
Wyoming	24	40	18	74
Ohio	24	23	26	294
Nebraska	25	38	22	246
Pennsylvania	25	41	22	302
Alabama	25	46	26	277
S. Carolina	26	32	21	229
Oklahoma	27	42	21	193
Minnesota	28	41	34	251
Idaho	28	36	19	97
N. Carolina	28	45	29	357
Texas	28	41	23	297
Virginia	29	40	24	373
Florida	30	44	18	438
Iowa	30	45	32	185
Indiana	30	44	18	185
Michigan	32	62	31	393
Illinois	35	51	23	361
Maryland	35	56	35	454
New Mexico	36	43	20	228
Massachusetts	37	50	45	472
Montana	37	46	25	298
Connecticut	38	52	29	444
Rhode Island	38	64	28	461
Delaware	39	49	27	502
Maine	40	51	42	282
Arizona	40	52	30	295

Table 23 *continued*

State	Percent Favoring Abortion All Cases	Percent Who Favor Government Funding	Percent Who Oppose Parental Consent	Ratio of Abortions to 1,000 Births, 1992
New York	40	70	38	694
Hawaii	41	56	25	617
Nevada	42	64	20	591
Vermont	42	57	41	393
Washington	42	54	39	447
Alaska	42	54	33	222
California	43	58	35	519
Oregon	44	47	44	372
New Hampshire	44	55	39	269
New Jersey	46	56	34	460
Colorado	48	54	32	362

levels of support for abortion in the public, although the abortion ratio was a bit higher (191).

The greatest support for government funded abortions is found in New York, where 70 percent of the respondents favored helping poor women who cannot afford an abortion. In contrast, Ohio residents were strongly opposed to providing government funds for abortions (only 23 percent in favor). Not surprisingly, the two states have very different Medicaid policies for abortion. Ohio provides Medicaid funding only when a woman's life is in danger. New York's law is more liberal, allowing for "medically necessary" abortions, which can include cases of fetal deformity, physical and psychological impairment (Weiner and Bernhardt 1990; NARAL 1992).

It is instructive to note that opinion on abortion is correlated with the metropolitan makeup of the fifty states. There is a significant and positive correlation between the percentage of people living in metropolitan areas and the mean public support score across all three abortion questions (Pearson Correlation coefficient = .35). The next section of this chapter explores the variation in abortion attitudes and presents a number of demographic variables that help account for the variation in support for abortion.

Explaining Variation in State Support for Abortion

A model accounting for abortion attitudes at the individual level was presented in chapter 4. The literature on abortion attitudes has documented the important influence of socioeconomic variables, religious variables, and sexual liberalism attitudes on abortion attitudes. At the state level, these individual level variables must be replaced by aggregate level variables that seek to model the same processes. For example, at the individual level, we have seen that people from higher socioeconomic backgrounds tend to be more supportive of abortion under any circumstance. At the aggregate level, we might expect the same process to be at work. Thus, we would expect to find states with more educated and higher paid citizens to be more supportive of abortion on demand. Thus, what we expect to find at the state level is an aggregation of the effects we find at the individual level.

Such an analysis is attempted here, using aggregate data for each state on five variables to explain the variation in support for abortion. The data include measures of income (median household income per capita in 1988), education (percentage of state residents with a college degree in 1980), urbanism (percentage of population living in metropolitan area, 1988), and religious variables (percentage of fundamentalist and Catholic adherents, 1980). All of these measures are used in multivariate regression equations to explain the variation in state support for the three NES abortion questions.

Many of these variables have been used in prior research to explain the variation in state policies on abortion (Goggin 1992; Goggin and Wlezien 1993; Guth and Halva-Neubauer 1993; Hansen 1980; Meier and McFarlane 1992, 1993; Tatalovich and Daynes 1989). The hypotheses suggested by the variables are that higher income states will have higher levels of support for abortion, higher support for government funding of abortion, and more liberal views toward parental consent laws. Likewise, states with higher levels of education will tend to have more liberal scores on the abortion questions. States with large urban populations are hypothesized as being more supportive of abortion rights. States with larger percentages of Mormon and fundamentalist adherents are expected to be more opposed to abortion. The measure of fundamentalist adherents serves as a surrogate indicator of the strength of fundamentalist adherents within each state, which have more conservative views on abortion (Guth and Halva-Neubauer 1993; Cook, Jelen, and Wilcox 1992).

The effect of Catholic populations on abortion opinion is uncertain. There is much debate on the impact this variable can have on abortion attitudes and abortion utilization (Guth and Halva-Neubauer 1993; Albritton and Wetstein 1991). Most scholars have modeled Catholicism in the states as a negative factor on abortion attitudes and abortion utilization. Yet the variable has produced confounding results in a number of studies (Hansen 1980; Berkman and O'Connor 1992; Albritton and Wetstein 1991). Several arguments might explain these mixed findings. First, the Catholic variable may be highly correlated with other variables, and thus reflect a spurious relationship. For example, high concentrations of Catholics tend to show up in highly urbanized, highly educated states. Thus, the strong correlation with these variables may be reflected in findings that report higher support for abortion in Catholic states

TABLE 24
Expected Impact of Variables on State Abortion Opinion

Variable	Percent Favoring Abortion in All Cases	Percent Favoring Government Funding	Percent Opposing Parental Consent
Percentage College	+	+	+
Median Income	+	+	+
Percentage Metropolitan	+	+	+
Percentage Fundamentalist	–	–	–
Percentage Catholic	?	?	?

(Albritton and Wetstein 1991). Second, though the official Church position on abortion is diametrically opposed to it under any circumstance, many Roman Catholics do not favor banning abortion (Guth and Halva-Neubauer 1993, 8). In other words, states that have high concentrations of Catholics also tend to have high concentrations of *ex-Catholics* and nonpracticing Catholics, many of whom have drifted from the church because of abortion and other church teachings. Thus, the impact of the percentage of Catholics in a state is left to reflect a two-tailed impact, with no direction implied. Table 24 is a summary of the expected effects of the variables on abortion opinion within the states.

With high collinearity between income and education, a factor score from principal components analysis was created to purge the negative effects such collinearity would have in multivariate regression equations (Berry and Feldman 1985). The variable is an index of the socioeconomic factors, using the standardized score for each state on a socioeconomic factor ranging from roughly –2 to +2.5, with higher scores representing higher socioeconomic levels. For example, Connecticut had the highest score on this variable (2.39); West Virginia received the lowest value (–1.95).

The results of a regression equation assessing the impact on support for abortion in all circumstances are presented in table 25. As expected, the percentage of fundamentalist adherents in a state had a significant, negative impact on support for abortion: for every increase of 5 percent in fundamentalists, there was a drop of one percent in support for abortion in all cases (.19 multiplied by 5 = .95, or roughly 1 percent). Higher socioeconomic status (SES) did produce a positive effect on public support for abortion. For every 1 point increase in the SES scale, there was an increase of just over 6 percent in support for abortion rights (b = 6.18). A small, insignificant negative effect turned up for the Catholic variable, with a decrease of 1 percent in abortion support for every 20 percentage point increase in Catholics. The metropolitan

TABLE 25
Regression Estimates: Support for Abortion in the States

Variable	b	Standard Error	Beta
Percentage Fundamentalist	−.19**	.08	−.28
Socioeconomic	6.18**	.66	.66
Percentage Catholic	−.05	.08	−.07
Percentage Metropolitan	−.01	.05	−.01
Constant	35.15	3.46	

adjusted R Square = .601
**significant at $p < .05$ or better

variable also failed to produce a significant impact when controlling for all other variables. The four variables do a decent job explaining the variance in support for abortion in the fifty states. The equation explains 60 percent of variance in the data (adjusted R Square = .601).

The regression equations explaining support for government funding of abortions and opposition to parental consent measures did not perform so well (tables 26 and 27). The amount of variance accounted for in the government funding equation drops to 38 percent (R Square = .377). This level of explanation is still robust and may reflect views on general conservative government spending patterns. The level of explanation falls even lower for the parental consent equation (R Square = .167). Thus, the variables identified here do a better job explaining the variation in support for abortion on demand than explaining support for government funding and opposition to parental consent laws.

Still, the percentage of fundamentalist adherents has a significant, negative effect on state attitudes on government funded abortions. For every 1 percent increase in fundamentalists, there is a drop of one-quarter percent in support for government funded abortions (b = −.24). Moreover, controlling for all other variables, the socioeconomic variable has a significant positive impact on

TABLE 26
Regression Estimates: Support for Government Funding

Variable	b	Standard Error	Beta
Percentage Fundamentalist	−.24**	.11	−.32
Socioeconomic	3.29**	1.61	.32
Percentage Catholic	.04	.11	.05
Percentage Metropolitan	.05	.06	.12
Constant	45.06	4.70	

adjusted R Square = .377
**significant at $p < .05$ or better

TABLE 27
Regression Estimates: Opposition to Parental Consent

Variable	b	Standard Error	Beta
Percentage Fundamentalist	−.09	.10	−.13
Socioeconomic	2.99**	1.42	.38
Percentage Catholic	.04	.09	.08
Percentage Metropolitan	.05	.06	−.13
Constant	31.22	4.15	

adjusted R Square = .167
**significant at $p < .05$ or better

support for government funding of abortions (b = 3.29). For every increase of 1 point on the socioeconomic scale, there is roughly a 3 percent increase in support for government funded abortions. Neither of the other two variables proved to have a significant impact on support for government funded abortions.

In the equation explaining opposition to parental consent measures, the socioeconomic variable is the only significant variable (table 27). For every 1 point increase in the SES scale, there is a 3-point increase in opposition to parental consent provisions. As in the previous equation, the percentage of Catholics has a positive effect on opposition to parental consent laws, although the impact is not significant in this equation.

These equations suggest that the strongest explanatory variables when accounting for variation in public support for abortion are measures of fundamentalism and socioeconomic structures of the states. Table 28 presents a series of equations using these two measures as independent variables to explain the variation in the three NES abortion questions, and a mean score calculated across the three questions. Both variables have a statistically significant effect on three of the measures of public support for abortion. In the parental consent equation, the fundamentalist variable does not have a significant effect, although the relationship is in the expected direction: more fundamentalists produces a negative influence on public opinion.

The importance of the analysis presented here is that it is the first systematic attempt to characterize variations in support for abortion in the fifty states. Although several studies have presented exploratory analyses, none attempts the scope presented here. For example, Norrander and Wilcox (1993) used only three variables to predict support for abortion in state publics, and none of their variables reflects a religious impact. Most researchers have been interested in explaining state policy variation and have devoted little attention to explaining state opinion from an aggregate perspective. The analysis presented here suggests that a measure of fundamentalism and an indicator of socioeconomic status of the states do a fairly good job predicting aggregate support for abortion.

TABLE 28
The Influence of Fundamentalism and Socioeconomic Levels
on Public Support for Abortion

DEPENDENT VARIABLE = Support for abortion in all cases

Variable	b	Standard Error	Beta
Percentage Fundamentalist	−.17**	.07	−.25
Socioeconomic	5.93**	.98	.63
Constant	33.46	1.36	
adjusted R Square = .614			

DEPENDENT VARIABLE = Support for government funded abortions

Variable	b	Standard Error	Beta
Percentage Fundamentalist	−.24**	.10	−.33
Socioeconomic	4.14**	1.34	.41
Constant	49.32	1.86	
adjusted R Square = .390			

DEPENDENT VARIABLE = Opposition to parental consent laws

Variable	b	Standard Error	Beta
Percentage Fundamentalist	−.12	.09	−.21
Socioeconomic	2.50**	1.18	.32
Constant	29.52	1.64	
adjusted R Square = .189			

DEPENDENT VARIABLE = Mean level of support across three questions

Variable	b	Standard Error	Beta
Percentage Fundamentalist	−.18**	.06	−.32
Socioeconomic	4.19**	.87	.54
Constant	37.43	1.21	
adjusted R Square = .554			

**significant at $p < .05$ or better

Moreover, when controlling for other variables, it is clear that Catholic populations in the states tend to favor pro-choice positions. States with larger concentrations of Catholics tend to be slightly more opposed to parental consent laws and more favorable toward government funding of abortions, even when controlling for socioeconomic factors, urbanism, and other religious denominations.

The analysis also echoes findings presented on individual attitudes presented in the previous chapter. While individual abortion attitudes are shaped by socioeconomic status and value structures that center on religious and moral beliefs, state aggregated analyses suggest that public opinion on abortion is shaped by the socioeconomic and fundamentalist composition of the mass public. Thus, aggregate public opinion on abortion in the United States mirrors attitude processes at the individual level. Since public opinion is the aggregation of thousands of individuals, we should not be surprised that forces at work at the individual level also appear at the aggregate level.

State Opinion and Policy on Abortion

Research on abortion policy has undergone an explosion in the late 1980s and early 1990s. Panels on abortion policy have been featured regularly at the annual meetings of the American Political Science Association and Midwest Political Science Association. The research culminated in the publication of a special issue of *American Politics Quarterly* on abortion in January 1993. Moreover, several new book-length treatments of abortion emerged in the early 1990s (Segers and Byrnes 1995; Byrnes and Segers 1992; Craig and O'Brien 1993; Goggin 1993; Cook, Jelen, and Wilcox 1992; Epstein and Kobylka 1992; Rosenberg 1991; Rosenblatt 1992; Staggenborg 1991; Tribe 1991). Clearly there has been a renaissance in abortion research in the 1990s.

Abortion policy has been the most active area of this revival of abortion research. Emerging out of that research are various indicators of abortion policy that have been developed to assess the variation in state policy. For example, Goggin and Kim (1992) have created a twenty-four-point index of state abortion policies by scoring state laws on a wide variety of indicators. Weiner and Bernhardt (1989) have used a seven-point scale to assess various state approaches to Medicaid funding of abortions. Halva-Neubauer (1990) has examined the legislative enactments of states in the wake of *Roe v. Wade* to codify states in a four-point typology of challenger, acquiescer, codifier, and supporter states. Albritton and Wetstein (1991) used a four-point index based on Medicaid provisions, parental consent laws, viability clauses, and declarations of legislative intent to overturn *Roe* to assess state policy approaches. Berkman and O'Connor (1992, 1993) created separate indices of Medicaid funding and parental consent laws for the states to measure state policy in two different ways, and Meier and McFarlane (1992, 1993) have computed a three-point scale based on a state's Medicaid funding policies.

Thus, a wide variety of indicators to measure abortion policy have emerged, with no one measure gaining universal acceptance. Three scales of policy are used for comparison in this chapter.[1] First, there is the Goggin and Kim (1992) twenty-four-point scale of 1988 abortion laws in the states. It represents the most comprehensive approach to measuring abortion policy and offers the widest

---

1. Measures of state abortion policy are discussed in a more systematic fashion in chapter 6.

amount of variation across the states. The scale simply sums the number of possible restrictions states have imposed on abortion, ranging from declarations of legislative intent to declare abortion unconstitutional (if the Supreme Court grants that authority) to restrictions on post-viability abortions. States that have the most restrictions placed on abortion rank closer to 24; states with fewer restrictions rank closer to zero.

A second measure of policy is a seven-point scale of Medicaid funding in the states (Weiner and Bernhardt 1990; Albritton and Wetstein 1991). It ranges from 1 to 7, with 1 representing the most restrictive Medicaid policy: allowing state funded abortions only to save the life of a woman. States that receive a score of 7 have the most liberal Medicaid policy, which allows Medicaid money to be used for any abortion. In between are states that limit Medicaid funding to cases in which fetal deformities are identified, for cases of rape and incest, or under conditions of psychological or physical harm.

A third measure of policy is a 1992 index of laws pertaining to minors' access to abortion (NARAL 1992, 147). This index ranges from 0 in states where minors face no legal barrier to abortion, to 5 in states where minors must get the consent of a parent or seek approval from a judge before obtaining an abortion. In between are (1) states that have enacted restrictions but do not enforce them because of legal injunctions; (2) states that require mandated counseling; (3) states that require parental notice with a judicial bypass option; and (4) states that require parental notification without a judicial bypass option. The measure is a good indicator of state policy approaches to limit access to abortions by minors.

Table 29 lists the states' scores on these three policy measures and provides a list of support for abortion in the mass public. States with higher measures of support for abortion tend to have fewer policy restrictions on abortion. For example, Colorado's mass public was most supportive of the abortion right (48 percent favored abortion in all cases), and its legislature has enacted only two abortion restrictions. Even with this high level of support for abortion on demand, Colorado does have a restrictive Medicaid policy, allowing for state funded abortions only when the woman's life is threatened. But Colorado is not alone in its approach to Medicaid funding; most of the states had similar policies for abortion in 1988 (NARAL 1989).

The opposite is true for a state like Kentucky, which has the lowest level of mass support for abortion under any circumstance (12 percent). Not surprisingly, Kentucky's abortion code is one of the most restrictive in the country, with fifteen restrictions on the books. Only four states had more restrictive laws in 1988: Illinois (16), North Dakota (17), Pennsylvania (17), and Missouri (18). In short, states that have low levels of support for abortion on demand tend to have more restrictive abortion laws and Medicaid policies. There is a significant negative association between public support for abortion and the number of

TABLE 29
Public Opinion and State Policies on Abortion, 1988–92

State	Percentage Who Favor Abortion in All Cases	1988 Number of Restrictions on Abortion in State (1–22)	1988 Medicaid Index for State (1–7)	1992 Index of Restrictions on Minors' Access (1–5)
Kentucky	12	15	1	1
W. Virginia	13	3	6	3
Mississippi	15	4	1	1
Arkansas	16	6	1	3
Missouri	19	18	1	5
N. Dakota	20	17	1	5
Louisiana	20	15	1	5
Wisconsin	22	5	3	2
Utah	22	14	1	4
Georgia	23	9	1	3
Kansas	23	2	1	0
Tennessee	23	11	1	1
S. Dakota	24	11	1	1
Wyoming	24	7	1	5
Ohio	24	5	1	3
Nebraska	25	10	1	3
Pennsylvania	25	17	2	1
Alabama	25	3	1	5
S. Carolina	26	5	1	5
Oklahoma	27	9	1	0
Minnesota	28	12	3	3
Idaho	28	11	1	1
N. Carolina	28	3	1	0
Texas	28	4	1	0
Virginia	29	5	4	0
Florida	30	9	1	0
Iowa	30	4	3	0
Indiana	30	8	1	5
Michigan	32	3	1	5
Illinois	35	16	1	1
Maryland	35	4	5	1
New Mexico	36	5	1	1
Massachusetts	37	12	7	5
Montana	37	9	1	1
Connecticut	38	1	2	2
Rhode Island	38	10	1	5
Delaware	39	6	1	1
Maine	40	6	1	2
Arizona	40	8	1	1

Table 29 *continued*

State	Percentage Who Favor Abortion in All Cases	1988 Number of Restrictions on Abortion in State (1–22)	1988 Medicaid Index for State (1–7)	1992 Index of Restrictions on Minors' Access (1–5)
New York	40	5	4	0
Hawaii	41	2	7	0
Nevada	42	11	1	1
Vermont	42	1	1	0
Washington	42	3	7	0
Alaska	42	2	7	1
California	43	5	7	1
Oregon	44	1	4	0
New Hampshire	44	2	1	0
New Jersey	46	4	7	0
Colorado	48	2	1	1

Sources: Halva-Neubauer 1990; Goggin and Kim 1992; Weiner and Bernhardt 1991; NARAL 1992

policy restrictions. The bivariate correlation between the two variables is −.42 (significant at .005).

It should also be noted that states that are most restrictive toward minors tend to cluster at the lower levels of support for abortion (top of table 28). Missouri, North Dakota, and Louisiana all have laws that score at the higher end of restrictions for minors, and this seems to match up well with levels of support for abortion in those states. In contrast, more pro-choice states tend to have fewer restrictions on minors (bottom of table 28).

Figure 10 displays the states' mean scores on the public opinion question and the twenty-four-point policy index on abortion. The figure allows one to visualize how greater support for abortion rights translates into fewer abortion restrictions. It also allows for better inspection of the variation in state policies and the states that do not fit the pattern very well. For example, West Virginia appears to be a unique case, with very few abortion restrictions, and yet, a very conservative mass public on abortion. West Virginia's House and Senate are said to be opposed to abortion as a legal option by "a wide margin" (NARAL 1989, 94). Despite this apparent consensus on abortion issues, legislators have failed to agree on abortion restrictions beyond a parental notification provision. State Medicaid guidelines allow for any abortion to be paid for by Medicaid funds, and the state legislative chambers have been unable to reach an agreement on Medicaid restrictions (NARAL 1989, 94–95). Mississippi has a similar pattern of opposition to abortion in the mass public and the legislature, yet retains a relatively liberal abortion law. Only four restrictions on abortion existed in 1988,

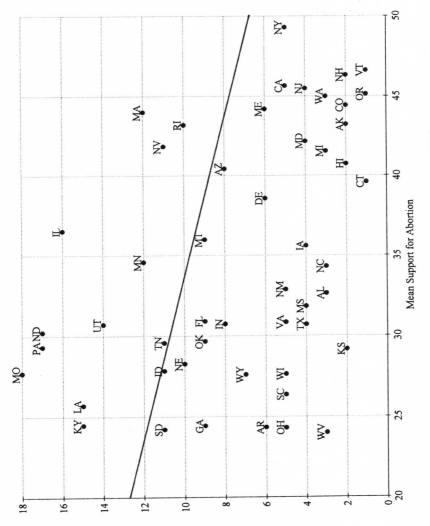

Figure 10. Abortion Policy Restrictions and Support for Abortion in the States, 1988

including a ban on all Medicaid funds for abortion, except to protect the life of the woman, and parental consent provisions (NARAL 1989, 51–52).

The anomalies represented by Mississippi and West Virginia may lie in past political leadership in the states. Both states have a history of Democratic party dominance in the state legislatures, although Mississippi's history is certainly more conservative (Barone and Ujifusa, 1989). Perhaps more important is top political leadership and its approach to abortion. In West Virginia, former Governor Jay Rockefeller was consistently pro-choice during the 1970s and early 1980s. Moreover, Attorney General Charles Brown was one of seven attorneys general to sign a pro-choice *amici curiae* brief in the *Webster* case (NARAL 1989, 94–95). In Mississippi, state politicians have simply avoided the abortion issue. For example, state legislators have not taken steps to repeal the pre-*Roe* law that criminalized the performance of abortions (NARAL 1989, 51). In response to NARAL questions, all of Mississippi's top politicians either refused to take a position or did not respond (NARAL 1989, 52).

Illinois represents another unique case among the states. There, public support for abortion is relatively high, with roughly 36 percent of the public favoring pro-choice responses on the NES questions. Yet the Illinois House and Senate have been actively involved in the effort to regulate abortion. In 1988, sixteen separate abortion restrictions were codified in Illinois law, including parental consent or notification, complete prohibition of Medicaid funds, a twenty-four-hour waiting period for minors, and a declaration of legislative intent to prohibit abortion in the event *Roe v. Wade* is overturned (NARAL 1989, 28–30). In Illinois, legislators appear to be more conservative than the mass public on abortion issues, and clearly more conservative than a string of pro-choice governors.

Despite these departures from patterns identified in the data, opinion on abortion does appear to have a significant impact on abortion policy. When examining the bivariate relationship between opinion and policy, state scores on abortion opinion account for 18 percent of the variance in the twenty-four-point policy index (R Square = .18). Moreover, the negative correlation coefficient suggests that for every 1-point drop in support for abortion, there is an increase of about 1 in the number of restrictions on abortion (b = −.84) in the states.

These findings are important because they give more weight to arguments that public opinion can have an impact on policy liberalism in the American states. Wright, Erikson, and McIver (1985, 1987; Erikson, Wright, and McIver 1993) have consistently demonstrated that liberal mass publics in the states translate into liberal policies in a wide variety of issue areas. The findings reported here mirror their research. States with liberal mass publics tend to have fewer restrictions on abortion and to have a greater likelihood of providing Medicaid funds for abortions.

6

Abortion Policy in the United States

The growing interest among political scientists in abortion research has produced numerous studies on abortion policy-making. Scholars have demonstrated the importance of previous abortion policies, demographic differences between the states, demographic composition of state legislatures, religious beliefs and personal characteristics of legislative members, and committee representation for abortion policy-making (Berkman and O'Connor 1992, 1993; Meier and McFarlane 1992, 1993; Tatalovich and Schier 1993; Eccles 1978; Vinovskis 1980; Witt and Moncrief 1993; Goggin and Kim 1992; Haas-Wilson 1993; Albritton and Wetstein 1991; Hansen 1980, 1993; Segers and Byrnes 1995). As indicated in the previous chapter, there is no agreement on the best measure of abortion policy. The result has been a wide range of dependent variables and the various independent variables that influence abortion policy.

The range of approaches to abortion policy indicate that different researchers seek different answers to different questions. In a recent review essay on the abortion literature, Malcolm Goggin (1993, 21) suggested that:

> Scholars need to clarify exactly what is meant by abortion policy and specify a measurement strategy that is appropriate to the unit of analysis.

The research presented in this chapter seeks to heed Malcolm Goggin's advice. Strategies for measuring abortion policy are presented, along with attempts to identify state level variables that shape those operationalizations of abortion policy.

Measurement of Abortion Policy

Berkman and O'Connor (1993, 121) have operationalized policy in two different ways: a three-point scale for parental notification and consent and a four-point scale for Medicaid funding (Hansen 1993). The Medicaid measure they use places states on a scale ranging from restrictive funding schemes (only to save the life of a woman) to funding abortion on demand. States scoring a 1 on parental notice and consent required parental consent in 1988; states scoring a 3 did not have any requirements. Similar dummy variable measures have been used by Deborah Haas-Wilson (1993) to demonstrate a statistical difference in abortion utilization between states with restrictive and permissive policies.

More importantly, Berkman and O'Connor (1993) contend that the two measures tap different factors in abortion policymaking. They indicate that the correlation between the Medicaid and parental consent measures is only .37, demonstrating rather convincingly that abortion policy can be properly modeled in very different ways. In short, abortion policies dealing with parental notice and consent seem to tap different factors than abortion funding schemes.

Berkman and O'Connor (1993) used these measures of policy to demonstrate that women legislators in the states have a significant influence on the shape of Medicaid funding policies and parental notification laws. Their research falls within a body of literature that has pointed out the different approaches women take toward policy-making in legislative bodies (Thomas 1991; Darcy, Welch, and Clark 1987; Thomas and Welch 1991). For example, Thomas (1991) has indicated that womens' political caucuses produce greater levels of interest in women, children, and family legislation in the states. Berkman and O'Connor (1993) contend that a "critical threshold" of women are needed to have an impact on abortion policy in the states. Their logged measure of Democratic women legislators leads them to claim that "the greater the number of women, the more likely the state will not require parental notification" (Berkman and O'Connor 1993, 111).

Meier and McFarlane (1993) used a similar Medicaid index divided into three groups of state policies. Voluntary unrestrictive states allow for abortion funding on demand. States that have been forced to provide Medicaid funds for abortion through court rulings are described as court order unrestrictive. Finally, other states generally limit Medicaid to abortions where the woman's life is threatened. States are scored from 2 to 0, with 0 representing the most restrictive funding policy (Meier and McFarlane 1993, 87–88).

Using a number of independent variables to explain state funding policy, Meier and McFarlane (1993) found that the number of National Abortion Rights Action League (NARAL) members in a state had a positive impact on their variable. Thus, the more pro-choice interest group supporters there are in a state, the more likely that state will have liberal funding policies. In contrast, Meier and McFarlane (1993, 88–92) found that greater percentages of Catholics in a state tended to deflate funding policies, leading to more restrictive Medicaid guidelines.

In a similar study, Susan Hansen (1993) suggested that funding restrictions in the states were best explained by the general policy approach toward women's issues, levels of access to abortion, and the general policy liberalism of the states. States that had higher levels of access to abortion and more liberal policy approaches tended to have fewer Medicaid restrictions (Hansen 1993, 238).

Other researchers have operationalized state policy on abortion in different ways. Weiner and Bernhardt (1989; Albritton and Wetstein 1991) used a survey of state Medicaid administrators (conducted in 1988) to develop a seven-point scale of Medicaid policies. This scale ranges from 1 to 7, with 1 representing states that provide funds only to save the life of the woman and 7 representing states that allow funding for any abortion. In between is a collection of states that allow funding for reasons of rape, incest, birth defects, and the possibility of physical and mental harm (Weiner and Bernhardt 1989). This scale differs slightly from indicators described by Berkman and O'Connor (1993), and Meier and McFarlane (1992, 1993), allowing for greater differentiation between state approaches.

Drawing a number of policy areas together, Albritton and Wetstein (1991) modeled state policies as an index of four indicators. They coded states on an additive scale, using dummy variable indicators of Medicaid restrictions, parental consent laws, post-viability restrictions, and legislative declarations of intent to prohibit abortion whenever possible. Their policy index helped account for much of the variance in access to abortion providers and also helped explain rates of abortion in the fifty states (Albritton and Wetstein 1991).

Several scholars have used an indicator of pre-*Roe* policy as a variable in models seeking to explain post-*Roe* variation in state policies (Hansen 1980, 1990; Halva-Neubauer 1990; Albritton and Wetstein 1991). The variable is generally operationalized in the spirit of table 2 (chapter 2), with unrestrictive states scored at one end, and states banning all abortions, except to save the life of the woman, at the other end. Note that abortion policy in this case serves as both a dependent and independent variable: abortion policy in 1972 is used as an indicator of a state's prior tendency to regulate abortion. Albritton and Wetstein (1991) have argued that the pre-*Roe* measure bears less relevance for studies today because states have moved so far beyond that era of abortion regulation.

Glen Halva-Neubauer (1990) examined state legislative enactments after *Roe v. Wade* to categorize states into four groups. His reading of state laws led him to describe challenger states as ones that: "repeatedly demonstrated hostility to *Roe*, through enactment of multiple pieces of anti-abortion legislation and a tenacious defense of these laws in federal court" (Guth and Halva-Neubauer 1993, 2). Codifier states enacted abortion restrictions, but only after court rulings that upheld the constitutionality of such provisions. Acquiescer states generally stayed away from the abortion debate but did enact a few restrictions. Finally, supporter states provided the greatest legal access to abortion and featured very few abortion restrictions (Halva-Neubauer 1990; Guth and Halva-Neubauer 1993). The breakdown of states according to Halva-Neubauer's (1990) scheme of policy enactments is provided in table 30.

Halva-Neubauer's (1990) categorization and measure of policy enactments is useful because it goes beyond presenting a snapshot of abortion policy at one point in time. The number of anti-abortion enactments serves as a measure of policy response over time at the state legislative level. Thus, it reflects policy

TABLE 30
Abortion Policy Enactments After *Roe v. Wade*,
Glen Halva-Neubauer's Categories of State Policy Response

Challenger States	Codifier States	Acquiescer States	Supporter States
Idaho (10)	Arizona (8)	Alabama (2)	Alaska (0)
Illinois (15)	California (5)	Arkansas (4)	Colorado (1)
Indiana (9)	Florida (8)	Delaware (4)	Connecticut (0)
Kentucky (13)	Georgia (8)	Iowa (4)	Hawaii (1)
Louisiana (12)	Maine (6)	Maryland (4)	Kansas (1)
Massachusetts (11)	Montana (7)	Michigan (3)	New Hampshire (1)
Minnesota (11)	Ohio (5)	Mississippi (3)	Oregon (0)
Missouri (13)	Oklahoma (7)	New Jersey (4)	Vermont (1)
Nebraska (9)	S. Dakota (8)	New Mexico (3)	Washington (1)
Nevada (9)	Virginia (5)	New York (3)	
N. Dakota (16)	Wisconsin (5)	N. Carolina (3)	
Pennsylvania (14)	Wyoming (7)	S. Carolina (2)	
Rhode Island (9)		Texas (3)	
Tennessee (11)		W. Virginia (2)	
Utah (14)			

Source: Glen Halva-Neubauer, "Abortion Policy in the Post-Webster Age," Publius: The Journal of Federalism (1990): 32. Reprinted by permission of the author and editor of the journal.

responsiveness in the 1973–1989 period and offers a current measure of abortion policy restrictions.

Another measure of policy resembling Halva-Neubauer's is the twenty-four-point index of abortion policy tabulated by Goggin and Kim (1992) and Goggin and Wlezien (1993). Covering every conceivable type of policy restriction that has been enacted, Goggin and Kim (1992; Goggin and Wlezein 1993) identified twenty-four different forms of abortion policy that have been codified into state laws. By simply totaling up the number of restrictions in each state law in 1988, these scholars developed the most detailed and varied measure of state abortion policy to date. Table 31 provides a listing of each state and the number of abortion restrictions recorded by Goggin and Kim and Goggin and Wlezein.

The twenty-four point index is not without flaws. For example, their recording of Medicaid provisions in state laws suggests that there is no variance in state Medicaid provisions. They indicate that all fifty states allow for Medicaid funds to save the life of a woman or for other medically necessary abortions. It would have been better to record states that provide Medicaid funds only for saving the woman's life as an abortion restriction. Moreover, several of

TABLE 31
An Index of Twenty-Four Abortion Policy Restrictions, 1988

Number of Restrictions	States (number)
18	Missouri (1)
17	N. Dakota, Pennsylvania (2)
16	Illinois (1)
15	Kentucky, Louisiana (2)
14	Utah (14)
13	(0)
12	Massachusetts, Minnesota (2)
11	Idaho, Nevada, S. Dakota, Tennessee (4)
10	Nebraska, Rhode Island (2)
9	Florida, Georgia, Montana, Oklahoma (4)
8	Arizona, Indiana (2)
7	Wyoming (1)
6	Arkansas, Delaware, Maine (3)
5	California, New Mexico, New York, Ohio, S. Carolina, Virginia, Wisconsin (7)
4	Iowa, Maryland, Mississippi, New Jersey, Texas (5)
3	Alabama, Michigan, N. Carolina, Washington, W. Virginia (5)
2	Alaska, Colorado, Hawaii, Kansas, New Hampshire (5)
1	Connecticut, Oregon, Vermont (3)

Sources: Goggin and Kim 1992; Goggin and Wlezien 1993; Halva-Neubauer 1989.

the regulations they list deal more with non-policy-making issues, such as sending memorials to Congress and clauses stating the intention to make abortion illegal if *Roe v. Wade* is ever overturned. Finally, the index assumes that all abortion restrictions carry equal weight, an assumption that is clearly off the mark. It is certainly the case that spousal and parental consent laws matter far more than non-binding clauses contained in statements of legislative intent.

Despite these drawbacks, the index does serve as a rough indicator of state approaches to abortion regulation. The additive scores provide a good account of the states we know to be active battlegrounds and testing grounds for abortion regulation. Note that Missouri (18) and Pennsylvania (17) receive high scores on the index. These two states were responsible for pivotal Supreme Court rulings in *Webster v. Reproductive Health Services* (1989) and *Planned Parenthood of Southeastern Pennsylvania v. Casey* (1992). It is also instructive to note that the least restrictive states have some of the highest abortion rates in the United States. California and New York, states with two of the highest abortion rates, have only five restrictions under the Goggin-Kim coding scheme. New York's provisions include a clause establishing viability between eighteen and twenty-four weeks, guidelines for post-viability abortions, second trimester hospitalization requirements, and Medicaid funding for medically necessary abortions. California's provisions include conscience clauses, a prohibition on fetal experimentation, post-viability requirements, Medicaid limitations, and parental consent restrictions.

Other studies have based models of abortion policy on the outcome of voting in legislative bodies. These studies focus on a different unit of analysis. While other researchers are interested in policy variation across the states, these researchers focus on individual representatives and the factors that influence their voting on abortion legislation (Eccles 1978; Vinovskis 1980; Daynes and Tatalovich 1984; Tatalovich and Schier 1993; Witt and Moncrief 1993; Wetstein and Ostberg 1993). Thus, policy in this sense is measured as a dichotomous outcome: whether a legislator supports a pro-choice position or not.

Generally, religious variables like Catholic, Protestant, or Mormon adherence have proven to be powerful predictors of legislators' votes on abortion bills (Tatalovich and Schier 1993; Daynes and Tatalovich 1984; Eccles 1978; Vinovskis 1980). Ideology, traditionally measured as a legislator's score on votes selected by Americans for Democratic Action (ADA), has also been a highly significant variable for congressional voting (Tatalovich and Schier 1993; Eccles 1978; Vinovskis 1980). Indeed, when controlling for a number of other variables, Vinovskis found that:

> A representative's overall liberalism is a much better predictor of the vote on restricting federal funds for abortions than any other variable, including the representative's religious affiliation. (Vinovskis 1980, 246)

Thus, more conservative members of Congress and state legislatures tend to vote against abortion funding and pro-choice positions.

Witt and Moncrief (1993) studied abortion voting in the Idaho state legislature to demonstrate the significant impact Mormon legislators can have on abortion policy-making. Nearly all of the Mormon legislators in 1990 (forty-one of forty-six) voted for a bill that would have placed significant restrictions on access to abortion (Witt and Moncrief 1993, 144). Protestant legislators were much more likely to oppose the bill in the Idaho legislature. Their research indicated that personal legislator characteristics were more powerful in predicting how legislators would vote than constituency variables that reflected the religious makeup of their districts (Witt and Moncrief 1993, 146–147).

Yet other researchers have found that constituency effects may influence voting at the U.S. Senate level (Wetstein and Ostberg 1993). In conjunction with individual Senator variables, measures of state variables like median household income, mass public opinion, percentage of Catholics, and relative access to abortion had significant impacts on abortion voting in the U.S. Senate through the 1978–1990 period (Wetstein and Ostberg 1993). For example, in states with greater access to abortion and a large concentration of abortion providers, 77 percent of the senators cast pro-choice votes. Likewise, in states with higher levels of median household income, 78 percent of the senators cast pro-choice votes (Wetstein and Ostberg 1993, 14–15). Moreover, principal components analysis of the variables they used demonstrated that individual and constituent level variables often load on the same factor. For example, an individual representative's ideology (ADA score) and state level measures of opinion liberalism (Wright, Erikson, and McIver 1987) both loaded strongly on an ideology factor (Wetstein and Ostberg 1993; Peltzman 1984). These findings find some evidence that constituency variables do matter in shaping legislator votes on abortion issues.

The approaches to abortion policy represent variations on a theme. Each of the indicators represents an interest in a different research question. Table 32 summarizes the various ways abortion policy has been characterized in the literature and the questions researchers have sought to address.

TABLE 32
Measurement of Abortion Policy and Research Questions

Authors	Measure	Research Question
Berkman and O'Connor; Hansen	Medicaid Index (1-4)	Explain state policy variation in Medicaid funding.
Meier and McFarlane	Medicaid Index (0-2)	Explain state policy variation in Medicaid funding and the rate of Medicaid funded abortions.
Weiner and Bernhardt; Albritton and Wetstein	Medicaid Index (1-7)	Explain state policy variation in Medicaid funding and abortion rates.
Haas-Wilson	Medicaid Dummy Variable (0-1)	Evaluate differences between states on abortion access and rates of utilization
Berkman and O'Connor	Parental Consent Index (1-3)	Explain state policy variation in parental consent and notice laws.
Haas-Wilson	Parental Consent/ Notification Dummy Variable (0-1)	Evaluate differences between states on abortion access and rates of utilization.
Albritton and Wetstein	Abortion Policy Index (1-4)	Explain state policy variation and abortion rates.

Table 32 *continued*

Authors	Measure	Research Question
Halva-Neubauer	Policy Enactment Index (0-16)	Explain policy-making responses of states in the wake of *Roe v. Wade*.
Goggin & Kim; Goggin & Wlezien	Abortion Policy Index (1-24)	Explain state policy variation.
Hansen, Albritton, and Wetstein	Pre-*Roe* Policy Index (1-5)	Explain post-*Roe* policy variation and abortion rates in the states.
Eccles, Vinovskis, Tatalovich, and Schier; Daynes and Tatalovich; Wetstein and Ostberg	Abortion Votes (0 or 1)	Explain individual voting of legislators on abortion issues.

Numbers in parentheses represent the minimum and maximum range of the indicators.

The Commonality of Abortion Policy Measures

Given the wide range in policy approaches identified in the literature, it may be instructive to settle the question of whether the various policy measures actually tap different factors. Berkman and O'Connor (1993) contend that Medicaid funding and parental notification are two different issues that fall under the umbrella of abortion policy-making. They back up their claim by pointing to the modest correlation between the two measures they used (Pearson correlation coefficient = .37). Yet a more reliable test of their claim would utilize factor analysis to see if the various measures of abortion policy load on different factors (Kim and Mueller 1978). If Berkman and O'Connor are correct, we would expect principal components analysis to yield more than one abortion policy factor.

Principal components analysis involving five of the measures discussed identified two separate factors among the policy indicators (table 33).[1] Three general indicators of policy and policy responsiveness loaded strongly on the first factor (the Goggin-Kim, Halva-Neubauer, and Albritton-Wetstein measures of policy). The 1988 policy index created by Goggin and Kim had a loading of .96, and the Halva-Neubauer measure (.94) and Albritton-Wetstein (.86) measures also produced robust factor loadings.

---

1. Varimax rotation was used to identify the two factors. The two factors explained 79 percent of the variance in the policy data. Both factors had Eigen values in excess of 1.0.

TABLE 33
Factor Loadings of Abortion Policy Measures:
The Commonality of Policy Measures

Variable	General Policy Factor	Medicaid Factor
Goggin-Kim (24-point)	.96	
Halva-Neubauer (16)	.94	
Albritton-Wetstein (4)	.86	
Weiner-Bernhardt Medicaid (7)		.66
Pre-*Roe* policy (5)		.87

Factor loadings are derived from a Varimax rotated factor solution. Loadings under .3 are omitted from the table.

The second factor appears to be a Medicaid funding factor, with the seven-point Medicaid scale loading strongly (.66), along with the five-point indicator of pre-*Roe* policy (.87). Thus, the Medicaid policy measure did load on a distinct factor, which is in line with the suggestion by Berkman and O'Connor (1993) that funding policies differ from other abortion restrictions.

The Halva-Neubauer measure of policy response correlates highly with the Goggin-Kim index of policies in 1988. The bivariate correlation between the two measures is .93, indicating once again that they essentially are the same measure of abortion policy in the states (table 34). Note that the pre-*Roe* measure of policy does not correlate strongly with any of the policy indices of 1988. Thus, pre-*Roe* policies have little relevance for studying contemporary abortion policies. As the 1973 ruling moves farther into history, its relevance for the variation in abortion policies in the present continues to wane. As Albritton and Wetstein (1991, 8) described it, "Pre-*Roe* policies matter less and less after *Roe*: what seems to matter is the *Roe* decision itself." This is reinforced by the fact that many states have allowed anti-*Roe* policies to remain in the statutes even though they are not enforced.

TABLE 34
Bivariate Correlations of Various Policy Indicators

	Halva-Neubauer	Albritton-Wetstein	Seven-point Medicaid	Pre-Roe Policy
Goggin-Kim	.93*	.79*	−.31	−.13
Halva-Neubauer		.72*	−.28	−.15
Albritton-Wetstein			−.53*	−.17
Seven-point Medicaid				.24

*significant at p = .001 or better

One flaw with all of these policy measures is that they are somewhat dated. In essence, they represent pre-*Webster* (or circa *Webster*) indicators of state policy approaches toward abortion. The farther we move away from the 1989 *Webster* decision, the less relevant they become for contemporary abortion policy research. In this chapter, three new policy indicators are presented to reflect abortion policies in the United States circa 1992 (NARAL 1992, 147–148). The policy measures are modeled after those utilized in the literature to this date.

One of the indicators was presented in the previous chapter, the index of state restrictions on minors' obtaining abortions at the start of 1992. The scale ranges from zero to five, with the most restrictive states having laws that require a teenager to get parental consent or a judge's approval. A second policy variable is modeled after Meier and McFarlane (1993) and Berkman and O'Connor's (1993) treatment of Medicaid funds for abortion. States are scored for their Medicaid approach at the beginning of 1992, with states allowing most or all abortions for indigent women to be paid for with Medicaid receiving a score of 0. The most restrictive states—ones that allow Medicaid funds to be used only when a woman's life is endangered—received a score of 3. States that also allowed Medicaid to be used for cases of rape or incest received a score of 2. States allowing for Medicaid funded abortions in cases of serious fetal defects received a score of 1. Finally, a third measure of policy adds the two scales together, providing an additive index (ranging from zero to eight) of state approaches toward parental consent and Medicaid funding. The ranking of states on the additive policy variable is provided in table 35.

The rest of this chapter is devoted to an attempt to explain as much of the variation in the three policy measures as possible, using independent variables that have been identified in prior research. More importantly, it is expected that the opinion measure derived from the previous chapter will play an important role in explaining the variation in abortion policies in the American states.

Explaining the Variance in State Abortion Policies

As indicated in the literature review described, a number of factors have been identified as playing an important role in shaping state abortion policies. This section identifies hypotheses to test using prior research and theory to guide the analysis. The important contribution added in this research is the inclusion of a measure of public support for abortion in the states—for the first time.

Women in State Legislatures

Some studies have emphasized the importance of women legislators in state policy-making (Thomas 1991; Thomas and Welch 1991; Kathlene 1992;

TABLE 35

State Policies Limiting Medicaid Funding and Access to Abortions by Minors, 1991

Policy Index		States (number)
0	Least Restrictive Policy	Hawaii, New Jersey, New York, N.Carolina, Oregon, Vermont, Washington (7)
1		Alaska, California, Iowa, Virginia (4)
2		Connecticut, Maryland (2)
3		Florida, Idaho, Kansas, New Hampshire, Oklahoma, Pennsylvania, Texas, W. Virginia (8)
4		Arizona, Colorado, Delaware, Illinois, Kentucky, Mississippi, Montana, Nevada, New Mexico, S. Dakota, Tennessee, Wisconsin (12)
5		Maine, Massachusetts, Minnesota (3)
6		Arkansas, Georgia, Nebraska, Ohio (4)
7		Utah, Wyoming (2)
8	Most Restrictive Policy	Alabama, Indiana, Louisiana, Michigan, Missouri, N. Dakota, Rhode Island, S. Carolina (8)

Source: National Abortion Rights Action League (NARAL), Who Decides? A State-by-State Review of Abortion Rights (*Washington, D.C.: NARAL, 1992, 147–148*).

Berkman and O'Connor 1993). Women legislators place more emphasis on women's issues in their legislative work, and once a critical threshold in the number of women legislators is passed, legislative successes follow (Thomas 1991; Berkman and O'Connor 1993). In addition, women legislators have been shown to be more pro-choice on abortion issues than their male counterparts (Darcy, Welch, and Clark 1987; Welch 1984; Berkman and O'Connor 1993; Richard 1995).

Given this support for a gender effect on abortion policy-making in prior research, any model of state policy variation should include a measure of the strength of women in legislative bodies. Several scholars have used a logged variable of the percentage of women serving in the legislature, arguing that a critical threshold must be met before women legislators have a significant impact on policy-making (Thomas 1991; Berkman and O'Connor 1993). In this study, several different operationalizations of this variable were attempted before settling on the percentage of women in the legislature in 1992. The simple percentage indicator was selected because it is easier to understand and interpret than the logged measure, and because the use of either measure produced similar statistical results.

Party Composition

A number of studies have pointed to the importance of Democratic party control for the enactment of liberal policies in the states (Wright, Erickson, and McIver 1987, 1993; Meier and McFarlane 1992, 1993; Berkman and O'Connor 1993). Three studies have demonstrated the impact this variable can have on abortion policy-making (Meier and McFarlane 1992, 1993; Berkman and O'Connor 1993). The hypothesis behind such an approach is that states controlled by the Democratic party will tend to support pro-choice legislation to a greater degree. Most state Democratic parties endorse pro-choice policies in their platforms (NARAL 1989, 1992).

The measure of party composition used here follows the lead of Berkman and O'Connor (1993). A proportion of Democratic party representation across the entire state legislature was created, dividing the total number of Democrats by the total number of seats in 1992. The proportion creates a scale from 0.0 to 1.0, with stronger Democratic states scoring closer to 1.[2]

Governors

With the power to veto legislation in forty-nine of the fifty states (North Carolina is the exception), governors have the potential to play a crucial role in shaping abortion policy. Where governors have a clearly stated pro-choice position, we would expect abortion policy to be in part influenced by the governor's position. For example, threats of a gubernatorial veto can have a profound influence on the shaping of abortion legislation. Thus, any model of variation in abortion policy should reflect the policy preferences of governors (Goggin and Kim 1992). In this study, governors' positions on abortion legislation were broken down into a dummy variable based on responses to a NARAL questionnaire (NARAL 1992). States in which governors voiced pro-choice positions were scored with a 1. States with governors who opposed pro-choice measures were scored with a 0. Again, the hypothesis is that states with pro-choice governors are more likely to have liberal abortion regulations.

Public Opinion on Abortion

Because of a paucity of data, public opinion on abortion has been missing from previous studies of abortion policy. Scholars have been left with two options. First, they could rely on surrogate measures of opinion like the opinion liberalism measure made famous by Wright, Erikson, and McIver (1985, 1987; Erikson, Wright, and McIver 1993), or aggregate scores on abortion opinion

---

2. Because Nebraska has a non-partisan, unicameral legislature, that state was coded with a score of .50 rather than being excluded from the analysis.

questions from surveys that did not feature random sampling frames (Albritton and Wetstein 1991). Moving away from public opinion, other researchers have relied on surrogate measures, such as membership in pro-choice interest groups (Berkman and O'Connor 1992, 1993) or congressional voting on abortion (Hansen 1980).

This study employs the public opinion measures discussed in chapter 5. Specifically, for the additive scale of abortion policy, it is hypothesized that greater support for abortion across the three NES questions will translate into fewer restrictions on abortion in the states. In reference to Medicaid policies, the greater the opposition to funding restrictions, the greater the access to Medicaid funds. The parental consent variable is matched up with the mean score for the NES question on parental consent policies. Keep in mind that this is the first direct test of public support for abortion on abortion policy.

Religion

Prior research suggests the number of Catholics, Mormons, and fundamentalists in a state can influence abortion policy-making (Berkman and O'Connor 1993; Meier and McFarlane 1992, 1993; Witt and Moncrief 1993; Guth and Halva-Neubauer 1993; Benson and Williams 1982; Erikson, Wright, and McIver 1993). Because of the Catholic Church's official opposition to abortion, it is hypothesized that the number of Catholics in a state will tend to dampen state legislative support for permissive abortion policies (Meier and McFarlane 1993; Berkman and O'Connor 1993). This dampening effect can either be the product of mobilized religious opposition in the states or the product of more Catholic legislators serving in the state legislatures. Additionally, the percentage of fundamentalist adherents in a state is hypothesized as having a negative effect on the enactment of pro-choice policies. Thus, greater levels of fundamentalist and Catholic adherents should lead to greater numbers of abortion restrictions.

The data for fundamentalist populations is taken from a 1980 survey of church membership published by the Glenmarry Research Center in Atlanta (Quinn et al. 1982). The denominations included in this fundamentalist variable are: Baptists, Latter Day Saints (Mormons), United Missionary, Church of God, Church of God in Christ, Nazarene, Plymouth Brethren, Pentecostal, Church of Christ, Salvation Army, Primitive Baptist, Seventh Day Adventist, and Missouri Synod Lutheran. The coding matches with data used by others, including Erikson, Wright, and McIver (1994, 65–67). The Catholic population data are taken from a 1990 national public opinion survey of religious identification conducted by Kosmin and Lachman (1991). The survey contacted 113,000 households in forty-eight states over a thirteen month period between April 1989 and April 1990. Data for Hawaii and Alaska are derived from the 1980 figures published by Quinn et al. (1982).

Pro-Choice Interest Group Support

In research explaining state abortion funding policies and parental consent laws, scholars have indicated that support for the National Abortion Rights Action League (NARAL) in the states has a tendency to positively influence liberal abortion laws (Meier and McFarlane 1992, 1993; Berkman and O'Connor 1993). The hypothesis behind this claim is that this variable reflects either pro-choice interest group mobilization within a state or greater public support for pro-choice positions. A similar measure is used in this study to test the impact NARAL membership can have.[3] The variable is the number of NARAL members per 10,000 residents of a state in 1988. Again, it is expected that larger NARAL membership will yield fewer abortion restrictions in the states.

Socioeconomic Variables

Wright, Erikson, and McIver (1985, 1987; Erikson, Wright, and McIver 1993) have demonstrated that one of the most powerful explanatory variables in comparative state policy research is the socioeconomic status of state residents. Wealthy and better educated state populations tend to have higher levels of welfare and social spending, and more liberal policy patterns (Wright, Erikson, and McIver 1985, 1987; Erikson, Wright, and McIver 1993; Albritton 1990; Luttbeg 1992).

In the abortion area, it has already been documented that states with better socioeconomic standing have more liberal views on abortion politics. Thus, it is expected that states with higher levels of socioeconomic status will have more permissive abortion policies and provide more Medicaid funding for abortions. The measure used to test this impact in this chapter is the same socioeconomic factor score discussed in chapter 4. It is the factor score for each state, from –2.0 to 2.5, developed from indicators of median household income and percentage of college educated citizens.

Southern Political Culture

State politics in the south have been shown to promote traditional values over other political values (Elazar 1984; Erikson, Wright, and McIver, 1993). Daniel Elazar's (1984) notion of traditional subcultures in the southern states suggests that legislators and the mass publics in those states approach abortion politics from a different perspective than in other states. Such states promote

---

3. I am grateful to Michael Berkman for providing the data on NARAL membership to me (after several unsuccessful attempts to acquire the data directly). Pro-life groups did not respond to several requests for membership data.

traditionally accepted modes of moral and social behavior, seeking to maintain certain standards of decency and order. As such, traditionalistic states would be expected to adopt more restrictions on abortion than states with other political cultures. To explore this hypothesis, a dummy variable is used to assess the impact of southern state political culture on abortion policy. States from the traditional deep south received a score of 1, and non-southern states were coded with a 0.

Method of Analysis and Results

Two separate regression equations were used on the three policy dependent variables: the index of policy toward minors in 1992, the index of 1992 Medicaid guidelines, and the additive policy index. First, a "political institutions" model was constructed to test the impact of institutional variables on abortion policies restricting access to minors (table 36, column 1). This model featured the NARAL membership variable, the percentage of women legislators, the Democratic ratio variable, the southern dummy variable, and the variable measuring a governor's position on abortion. A second equation tested the impact of demographic variables on policy, including public opinion, socioeconomic factors, and religious variables (table 36, column 2). This model featured the state opinion score, the socioeconomic scale, and the two religious variables (percentage of Catholic and fundamentalist adherents).

The regression equation modeling institutional effects did a poor job explaining the variance in the six-point index of restrictions on minors. The four institutional variables explained only 10 percent of the variance in the policy index (adjusted R Square = .096). The only significant variables in the equation were the dummy variable for the governor's position on abortion and the percentage of women in the state legislature. The regression coefficients indicate that states with a pro-choice governor will have on the average one less restriction on minors (b = −1.08), while states with greater percentages of women in the state legislature will have fewer restrictions (b = −.07). Two of the other variables, proportion of Democrats and strength of pro-choice interest groups, have virtually no impact on this policy measure. When controlling for other variables, the southern variable actually has an unexpected impact on abortion policy. The negative coefficient for the southern dummy variable implies that southern states have fewer restrictions on minors when controlling for other institutional factors.

The demographic model does a much better job explaining variation in the policy toward minors (adjusted R Square = .140; table 36, column 2). Two of the variables have a significant effect on the policy score: the socioeconomic variable (b = −.61) and the Catholic variable (b = .06). These coefficients suggest that states with higher socioeconomic levels have fewer abortion

TABLE 36
Regression Estimates of Policy Restrictions on Minors:
The Impact of Institutional and Demographic Variables

Variable	Institutional Model	Demographic Model—1	Demographic Model—2	Combined Model
Percentage of Women Legislators	−.07*			−.03
	(.04)			(.03)
Governor's position	−1.08**			−.70
	(.54)			(.53)
Proportion Democrats	.03			
	(.02)			
NARAL Members	.00			
	(.01)			
Southern Culture	−1.01			
	(.74)			
Public Opinion—Consent		−.02		
		(.04)		
Mean Public Support			−.07*	−.08*
			(.05)	(.04)
Socioeconomic Factor		−.61*	−.40	
		(.34)	(.37)	
Percentage Fundamentalist		.04	.03	
		(.02)	(.02)	
Percentage Catholic		.06**	.06**	.04**
		(.02)	(.02)	(.02)
Constant	2.57	.58	2.41	4.85
	(1.45)	(1.31)	(1.89)	(1.13)
R Square	.188	.210	.239	.233
adjusted R Square	.096	.140	.171	.164

unstandardized regression coefficients
numbers in parentheses are standard errors
**significant at p = .05, *significant at p = .10.

restrictions on minors, and states with greater concentrations of Catholics have more restrictions. While the opinion variable is not significant, its effect is in the expected direction: where support is higher in mass publics, there are fewer abortion restrictions facing teenagers (b = -.02). The fundamentalist variable also has a regression coefficient in the expected direction (b = .04).

The third column in table 36 uses the mean opinion score on abortion rather than the specific opinion score on the question dealing with parental consent. In other words, the impact of general abortion attitudes across a set of questions is measured instead of the direct policy related question. Note that when using this variable, general public opinion on abortion has a significant effect on this measure of abortion policy (b = –.07, significant at the 90 percent confidence level). The Catholic variable remains significant, while the socioeconomic variable is no longer significant. The fourth column in table 36 combines the significant variables in columns 1 and 3 to create a combined model to explain policy restrictions. In this case, the demographic variables measuring public support for abortion (b = –.08) and levels of Catholicism (b = .04) play a much stronger role in explaining policy variation. The political institutional variables fail to have a significant effect on this measure of abortion policy, although their influence is in the expected direction.

It is important to note that the opinion variable, representing the mean level of pro-choice support, has a significant influence in explaining the abortion policy index pertaining to minors (b = –.08 in the combined equation). This is significant because it implies a strong connection between public opinion on abortion and abortion policy in the states. Indeed, even when controlling for religious concentrations in the states, the effect of opinion is significant. This is yet another validation of the thesis that public opinion has a role in explaining state policy differences (Wright, Erikson, and McIver 1985, 1987; Erikson, Wright, and McIver 1993).

The institutional variables do not perform any better in accounting for the variance in the seven-point Medicaid index (table 37, column 1). The four variables account for only 8 percent of the variance in the Medicaid policies. None of the variables proves to be significant. However, the influence of most of the variables is in the expected direction: pro-choice governors, greater percentages of women in the legislature, and higher proportions of Democrats are associated with fewer Medicaid restrictions. Thus, greater numbers of women and Democrats in state legislatures, and pro-choice governors tend to translate into greater access to Medicaid funding for abortions. The southern dummy variable is in the expected direction as well, with southern states tending to have more restrictions on Medicaid funded abortions. The interest group variable again failed to provide any significant explanatory power.

The demographic equation has much more explanatory power but is dominated by the socioeconomic variable (table 37, column 2). The variable suggests that states with wealthier and better educated citizens have fewer Medicaid restrictions (b = –.69). The impact of the opinion variable modeling support for Medicaid funded abortions is in the expected direction, but not significant. Similarly, the impact of the religious variables is in the expected direction, but only the Catholic variable is significant (b = .03). The first

TABLE 37
**Regression Estimates of Medicaid Restrictions:
The Impact of Institutional and Demographic Variables**

Variable	Institutional Model	Demographic Model—1	Demographic Model—2	Combined Model
Percentage Women Legislators	−.03 (.03)			−.01 (.02)
Governor's position	−.57 (.37)			−.12 (.34)
Proportion Democrats	−.02 (.01)			
NARAL Members	.01 (.01)			
Southern Culture	.56 (.51)			
Public Opinion—Medicaid		−.02 (.02)		
Mean Public Support			−.04 (.03)	
Socioeconomic Factor		−.69** (.22)	−.59** (.23)	−.79** (.21)
Percentage Fundamentalist		.01 (.02)	.01 (.02)	
Percentage Catholic		.03* (.01)	.03* (.01)	.02 (.01)
Constant	3.55 (1.00)	1.92 (1.06)	2.64 (1.18)	1.83 (.59)
R Square	.172	.350	.367	.324
adjusted R Square	.078	.292	.311	.264

unstandardized regression coefficients
numbers in parentheses are standard errors
**significant at p = .05, *significant at p = .10.

demographic model explains about a third of the variance in the Medicaid index (adjusted R Square = .292). The second demographic model replaces the opinion variable on Medicaid funds with the mean support score (table 37, column 3). The equation is similar to the first demographic model: mass support has the expected impact on abortion policy but is not significant, while the socioeconomic variable has the most explanatory power. It should be noted that using the mean support score boosts the explanatory power of the demographic equation slightly (adjusted R Square = .311).

When the significant variables from the institutional and demographic equations are combined, the variable measuring socioeconomic status has the only significant impact on Medicaid policy. All of the other variables have the expected impact but are insignificant. The combined effect of the four variables explains a quarter of the variance in the Medicaid index (adjusted R Square = .264). The equations presented here suggest that state Medicaid policies are largely influenced by the socioeconomic structures of the states. Since the policy in question is a government funding policy, it is not surprising that the most important variable influencing the dependent variable taps the relative wealth of the states.

Table 38 features regression estimates of the combined nine-point index of abortion policy (combining parental consent and Medicaid approaches). Once again, the demographic model does a far better job in explaining policy variation in the states. In the institutional model, the pro-choice governors and greater percentages of women in the legislatures produced fewer abortion restrictions (b = –1.64 and –.10 respectively). None of the other variables proves significant. In the demographic model, three variables are statistically significant: the socio-economic and Catholic variables are significant at the 95 percent confidence level, and the public opinion variable is significant at the 90 percent confidence level. The coefficient for the public opinion measure indicates that as support for pro-choice positions goes up by 10 points in the states, the policy score drops by 1 point (b = –.11). This effect occurs even in the face of controls for socio-economic levels, the percentage of Catholics, and two institutional variables (table 38, column 3). This means that public support for abortion has a signifi-cant effect on the shape of policy toward abortion, even in the face of political, religious, and socioeconomic variables. This finding has never been documented directly and has only been hinted at in prior research on abortion policy.

Abortion Policy and Abortion Rates

While it is important to know the variables that account for state differences in abortion policy, it is also important to know how those policy differences affect abortion utilization. Specifically, do policy differences help explain the differences in abortion rates in the states?

A simple direct test of this research question is to examine the bivariate correlations between policy measures and abortion rates. None of the policy measures discussed in this chapter has a significant bivariate correlation with abortion ratios per 1,000 live births in the states. For example, the Goggin-Kim index of policy had only a –.11 correlation with the 1989 abortion ratio per 1,000 live births. The Medicaid index had a higher correlation (r = .32), but was

TABLE 38
Regression Estimates of Nine Point Policy Index:
The Impact of Institutional and Demographic Variables

Variable	Institutional Model	Demographic Model	Combined Model
Percentage Women Legislators	−.10**		−.03
	(.05)		(.04)
Governor's position	−1.64**		−.60
	(.74)		(.68)
Proportion Democrats	.01		
	(.03)		
NARAL Members	.00		
	(.01)		
Southern Culture	−.44		
	(1.01)		
Mean Public Support		−.11*	−.11*
		(.06)	(.06)
Socioeconomic Factor		−.98**	−.96**
		(.46)	(.47)
Percentage Fundamentalist		.04	
		(.03)	
Percentage Catholic		.09**	.07**
		(.03)	(.03)
Constant	6.12	5.05	6.96
	(1.99)	(2.31)	(1.98)
R Square	.201	.403	.396
adjusted R Square	.111	.349	.327

unstandardized regression coefficients
numbers in parentheses are standard errors
**significant at p = .05, *significant at p = .10.

still not significantly correlated with abortion rates. However, the nine-point
index of policy in 1992 is significantly correlated with abortion ratios in 1992 (r
= - .45, significant at .01). Relying on these correlations, we would have to settle
for mixed results from our direct test.

These mixed results are not puzzling if policy is correlated with measures
of access to abortion. Thus, abortion policy might have indirect effects on
abortion rates through the amount of access to abortion. Liberal abortion policies
would be expected to engender more interest in clinics and hospitals offering

abortion services. The causal relationship runs along the following lines: abortion policy affects access to abortion, and access to abortion affects abortion rates. Thus, we would expect strong correlations between abortion policy and indicators of access to abortion, and strong correlations between indicators of access to abortion and abortion rates.

In the literature, access to abortion has traditionally been measured by the percentage of hospitals offering abortion services in each state (Tatalovich and Daynes 1989; Hansen 1980). With increasing percentages of abortions being offered in clinics and outpatient centers (as many as 85 percent), this measure has become suspect. Moreover, the percentage of hospitals does not reflect any sense of the burden faced by women who must travel great distances in states where clinics are not abundant (Gorney 1990; Henshaw and Van Vort 1990). In both North and South Dakota, only one abortion provider existed in 1992 (Henshaw and Van Vort 1990, 1994).

A better measure of access to abortion would feature the percentage of counties in each state that have an abortion provider (Gorney 1990; Henshaw and Van Vort 1994). Table 39 correlates this measure of access (percentage of counties with a provider in 1988) with the 1988 policy measures discussed previously. The table also features the abortion ratio variable and the percentage of hospitals in each state that performed abortions in 1985 (Tatalovich and Daynes 1989).

First, it is important to reiterate that neither of the policy measures correlates strongly with the abortion ratio measure. Yet the two policy indices do correlate significantly with the indicators of access. The twenty-four-point index of policy restrictions has a significant negative correlation with the percentage of counties (−.37) and hospitals (−.51) providing abortion services. Thus, where there are more restrictions on abortion, there tend to be fewer abortion providers. Similarly, where there are more permissive policies on Medicaid funded abortions, there is greater access to abortion.

TABLE 39
Abortion Policy and Abortion Rates; Bivariate Correlations, 1988

Variable	Goggin-Kim Twenty-Four-point Policy	Albritton-Wetstein Medicaid	Percentage Counties	Percentage Hospitals
Abortion Ratio	−.11	.32	.65**	.58**
Twenty-Four-point Policy		−.31	−.37*	−.51**
Seven-point Medicaid			.50**	.55**
Percentage Counties				.81**

**significant at .001, *significant at .01

Both access measures have strong positive correlations with abortion ratios. Indeed, the bivariate correlations suggest that the percentage of counties with abortion providers can explain 42 percent of the variance in abortion ratios (.65 squared = .42). This strong impact of access to abortion echoes research reported by Hansen (1980), and Tatalovich and Daynes (1989).

The next chapter details a more complex model of abortion rates in the United States, tying together the various strands that have been discussed so far. What is important to note from this preliminary analysis of policy is that abortion rates can be influenced directly and indirectly by key variables. While policies do not appear directly to influence abortion rates, they do have a profound impact on the level of access women have to abortion. And it is the level of access that matters most when explaining the differences in abortion rates in the American states.

Conclusion

When examining the impact of institutional variables alone, measures tapping the position of governors on abortion issues and the power of women legislators tend to demonstrate an important effect on abortion policy. The research reported here indicates that once a critical threshold of women legislators is reached, states tend to have more permissive abortion policies and more generous Medicaid guidelines for abortion. This finding reinforces arguments presented by scholars who have sought to examine the influence women can have in setting new legislative priorities and focusing on women's issues (Thomas and Welch 1991; Thomas 1991; Darcy, Welch and Clark 1987).

Yet the variance in abortion policy in the states is not well accounted for by institutional variables. Indeed, demographic factors that model the religious and socioeconomic makeup of the states do a much better job explaining variations in state abortion policy. This finding, coupled with the fact that opinion on abortion issues is strongly tied to abortion policy, argues for a comprehensive explanation of abortion policy. It is not enough to examine state legislatures and their makeup, and it is not enough to gauge interest group strength in the states. More often than not, those factors are shaped by the social, economic, religious, and opinion climate within the states.

Finally, we must go beyond abortion policy to determine how it shapes access to abortion, and ultimately, the utilization of abortion by women It is not enough to explain state differences on abortion policy without tying policy to its impact on the decisions women have to make. Ultimately the variation in state policies leads to variations in access to abortion. These findings suggest that any model seeking to explain abortion rates in the American states should account for a complex sequence of direct and indirect effects through state policies and access to abortion. Such a model is presented in the next chapter.

7

Explaining Abortion Rates in the United States

Up to now, this book has focused on policy change and its influence on abortion rates, the structure of attitudes on abortion, the factors that explain support for abortion in the states, and the various factors that influence state policy on abortion. These findings have prepared the way for a multivariate analysis of abortion rates in the American states.

Since 1980, Susan Hansen's study has stood as the defining research on the differences of abortion rates in states. Her seminal work outlined the structures of variation in abortion utilization in 1976. For example, Hansen (1980) found that greater access to abortion led to higher abortion rates. Likewise, more permissive Medicaid policies also engendered higher abortion rates. Hansen (1980) also found that states with larger urban populations have higher abortion rates. She used a number of policy, access, and demographic variables to explain 72 percent of the variance in state abortion rates (Hansen 1980, 390).

Much has changed in the abortion arena since Hansen's publication. As previous chapters have demonstrated, the devolution of abortion policy to state governments through a series of Supreme Court decisions has brought a wide variety of state regulations to the abortion policy domain. The federal government cut off federal Medicaid money to pay for most abortions in 1978. Recently the Clinton Administration altered the policy to require states to provide funds in cases of rape and incest. Not surprisingly, the policy change has attracted several legal challenges from states that tend to oppose governmental funding schemes. Since *Roe,* a number of states have sought to restrict access to abortion through more stringent regulation. In short, the policy arena that existed under Hansen's research no longer applies to abortion utilization in the 1990s. For that reason, an update of the structures of abortion use in the American states is called for.

More importantly, little has been done to explore the relevance of public opinion for abortion access. Indeed, in Hansen's work, public opinion was excluded from the explanatory variables because "survey data are not available for every state" (Hansen 1980, 386). In place of public opinion, Hansen used measures of legislative support for the Hyde Amendment in Congress. Such an approach seems inappropriate for the late 1980s and early 1990s, when abortion policy became the domain of state policymakers. New sources of data for public opinion on abortion make this connection to policy and abortion utilization possible for the first time.

This chapter ties together many of the strands discussed in this study so far. A structural equation model is presented to explain the impacts of a number of variables on abortion rates in the American states. The importance of this model is its inclusion of public opinion on abortion and its refinement of Hansen's 1980 research. The expected direction of effects that variables will have on abortion rates is laid out in the introductory section, with results and path coefficients reported in the second section.

Independent Variables and Hypotheses

The dependent variable here is the ratio of abortions to 1,000 live births reported for each state in 1992. Data on all the independent variables come from that same year or just prior to 1992. For example, the public opinion measure is the mean abortion support score for each state from the NES Senate Panel Studies of 1988 and 1990 discussed in chapter 5. The other independent variables and their expected effect on abortion rates are discussed below.

Access

Access to abortion services in the states has been the most important factor influencing past abortion rates (Hansen 1980; Tatalovich and Daynes 1989; Henshaw and Van Vort 1987). The correlation between the percentage of hospitals offering abortion services and abortion rates in 1975 was .71 (Hansen 1980, 383). Similar associations for the same variables were reported by Tatalovich and Daynes (1989) in the late 1980s (r = .72).

The declining number of hospital abortion providers makes an access measure rooted in hospitals performing abortions suspect. With nearly 90 percent of all abortions obtained in clinics and physicians' offices, a new measure of access is needed (Tatalovich and Daynes 1989). In the previous chapter, access to abortion was measured as the percentage of counties in a state that had at least one abortion provider in 1988. This indicator is a better reflection of access because it better reflects the contemporary nature of access to abortion in clinics.

The percentage of counties offering abortions is highly correlated with state abortion rates. In any causal model explaining abortion rates, we would expect a strong positive impact from this measure of access: the greater the percentage of abortion providers in a state, the greater the number of abortions.[1]

State Policies

This study demonstrates that state policies on abortion are inversely correlated with access to abortion services. States with more abortion restrictions tend to have fewer abortion providers. Thus, a causal model of abortion rates would imply an indirect impact of state policies on abortion rates through the intervening variable of access to abortion providers. As indicated earlier, greater restrictions means fewer providers, which means fewer abortions. The measure of state policy used in the causal model is the nine-point index of policy restrictions facing minors and adult women seeking Medicaid funding.

Institutional Variables

Institutional variables model the impact that state legislatures, governors, and interest groups can have on abortion policy. Much of the theoretical justification for these variables was presented in chapter 6. The variables include the governor's position on abortion issues, the percentage of women serving in the legislature, the percentage of Democrats serving in the legislature, and the number of NARAL members in the state. Institutional variables are expected to influence abortion rates in an indirect way, through their impact on abortion policy restrictions. Thus, the causal chain runs something like the following: Where institutional factors favor abortion rights, there will be fewer policy restrictions, greater access to abortion, and higher abortion rates. All of these institutional variables are described in chapter 6.

Public Opinion

In theory, mass publics that tend to favor abortion rights are more likely to elect legislators and representatives who share their views. In practice, only a small minority of voters use abortion as an issue that decides their vote in elections (Center for Governmental Studies 1989). Yet some scholars maintain that abortion is becoming increasingly important in isolated state elections. For example, recent New Jersey and Virginia gubernatorial elections prominently

1. Of course this measure of access does not tap another intriguing feature that influences access to abortion: the distance traveled by women to obtain abortions. Gorney (1990) has indicated that women in South and North Dakota must travel great distances to reach the sole abortion provider in each state. Dr. Lettie Wenner has suggested an avenue for future research is to calculate access based on the number of providers per square mile in each state.

featured debates over abortion policy (Dodson and Burnbauer 1990). Recent referenda in several states have also demonstrated the mass public's willingness to reject abortion restrictions (Segers and Byrnes 1995). Even if abortion is not used as an important issue in elections, policies in the states do match well with aggregate attitudes on abortion.

Research presented in this study suggests that public opinion does correlate strongly with state abortion policies. The causal hypothesis is that where support for abortion is strong, state policies will reflect fewer restrictions, access to abortion will be greater, and abortion rates will be higher. In contrast, lower levels of support for abortion will translate into greater restrictions on abortion, lower levels of access, and lower abortion rates. The NES measure of support for abortion is used in the following analysis.

Religious Variables

In Hansen's (1980) study of abortion rates, the percentage of Mormons in the states had a direct, negative impact on abortion rates. Such a finding is not surprising, given the cultural and political differences where Mormons predominate (Albritton 1990; Witt and Moncrief 1993). Similar findings are likely in states with large concentrations of fundamentalist and Pentecostal adherents (Cook, Jelen, and Wilcox 1992). In past studies, large concentrations of Catholics have also been expected to influence abortion rates negatively (Hansen 1980; Tatalovich and Daynes 1989).

The working hypotheses for religious variables, therefore, resemble the following: For fundamentalists, it is expected that a direct negative effect will exist between fundamentalists and abortion rates. Fundamentalist populations also have the potential to indirectly influence abortion rates through their impact on policy and public opinion. The percentage of Catholics in a state is expected to have indirect impacts on abortion rates through its effects on abortion policy in the states and on public opinion. The measures used in this model are the same ones discussed in chapter 5.

Urbanization and Socioeconomic Variables

A strong association can be found between abortion rates and the percentage of people living in metropolitan centers (Hansen, 1980, 383). Because abortion providers are largely concentrated in metropolitan centers, it is not surprising to find correlations as high as .60 between abortion rates and measures of metropolitan population (Hansen 1980, 383; Tatalovich and Daynes 1989; Henshaw and Van Vort 1990; Powell-Griner and Trent 1987). States with large metropolitan areas also require less individual travel to an abortion provider, and rural states have fewer abortion providers (Henshaw, Koonin, and Smith 1991; Henshaw 1991; Gorney 1990).

A causal model of abortion rates must therefore account for the concentration of abortion providers in urban states. Theoretically, abortion providers locate where demand for abortion is highest (Medoff 1988). Thus, states with high population levels in metropolitan areas are expected to have greater access to abortion and higher abortion rates. The measure used here is the percentage of the population in each state that lived in a metropolitan area in 1992 (as defined by the U.S. Census Bureau designation of a Standard Metropolitan Statistical Area [SMSA]).

Similarly, states with greater levels of median income and education have proven to be more supportive of abortion. Higher socioeconomic status leads to a more supportive mass public on abortion issues. In a causal model of abortion rates, socioeconomic variables should have an indirect influence through aggregate measures of public support for abortion. The socioeconomic indicator used in this analysis is the socioeconomic factor score for each state discussed in chapter 5.

Controlling for Demand

Abortion rates have been found to be higher among unmarried women in the United States (Henshaw and Van Vort 1994; U.S. Centers for Disease Control 1993). For example, the rate of abortion per 1,000 married women aged fifteen to forty-four was 9.2 in 1987 and 45.6 for unmarried women (Henshaw, Koonin, and Smith 1991, 76). Thus, states that have higher concentrations of households with unwed residents are likely to have higher levels of demand for abortion. Any model of abortion rates should take this factor under consideration. In this study, a simple measure of demand is utilized: the percentage of households with unmarried residents in each state. The hypothesis is that as this variable increases, the number of abortion providers should increase, and abortion rates should be higher.

A visual display of the expected effects each variable will have on the abortion rates of states is presented in table 40. Note that the policy index measure is the number of restrictions on abortion, which means that greater support for abortion in the mass public should have a negative effect on the policy variable. Taking the metropolitan variable as an example, we would expect it to have a positive impact on support for abortion, a negative impact on policy restrictions, a positive impact on access to abortions, and a positive indirect effect on abortion rates.

A structural equation model was developed to estimate the effects of the variables simultaneously on abortion rates, access to abortion, abortion policy, and public support for abortion. The equations were developed from previous research and findings reported in earlier chapters of this book. For example, the equation explaining policy in 1992 was expected to include significant variables

TABLE 40
The Expected Effects of Variables in a Causal Model of Abortion Rates

Variable	Abortion Rates	Access to Abortion	Abortion Policy	Public Support
Percentage Counties	+			
Policy Index	−	−		
Percentage Unmarried	+	+		
Public Support	+	+	−	
Governor Position	+	+	−	
Proportion Democrat	+	+	−	
Percentage Women	+	+	−	
NARAL Members	+	+	−	
Percentage Metropolitan	+	+	−	+
Percentage Fundamentalist	+	−	+	−
Percentage Catholic	−	−	+	+
Socioeconomic Factor	+	+	−	+

from the combined institutional and demographic model: public support for abortion, percentage of Catholics, and the socioeconomic variable. Likewise, the opinion equation features the two significant variables from the equation presented in chapter 5: percentage of fundamentalists and the socioeconomic variable.[2]

Bivariate Correlations and Regression Results

To test the direction of the expected effects, bivariate correlations were explored first. Table 41 presents the bivariate relationships between the independent variables and abortion rates, abortion access, abortion policy, and public support for abortion. The table essentially replicates table 40, replacing positive and negative signs with the actual bivariate correlations between variables, and also serves as a review of some of the findings presented so far.

Nine of the variables have significant correlations with the abortion rate variable: the access variable (.73), the policy index (−.45), public support for abortion (.70), percentage metropolitan (.66), percentage Catholic (.41), the socioeconomic measure (.67), the measure of fundamentalism (−.51), percentage

---

2. The institutional variables, having not performed well in explaining the policy index, were omitted from the causal model presented here. This is not to imply that institutional factors do not impact abortion rates. This model merely presents a parsimonious explanation of direct and indirect effects on abortion rates using a number of variables, which do a better job accounting for the variance than the institutional variables.

TABLE 41
Bivariate Correlations of Independent Variables
With Abortion Rates, Access, Policy, and Public Support

Variable	Abortion Rates	Access to Abortion	Abortion Policy	Public Support
Percentage Counties	.73**			
Policy Index	−.45**	−.46**		
Percentage Unmarried	.68**	.34		
Public Support	.70**	.70**	−.49**	
Governor Position	.46**	.43*	−.32	
Proportion Democrat	.20	.11	.04	
Percentage Women	.11	.26	−.32	
NARAL Members	−.05	−.13	.00	
Percentage Metropolitan	.66**	.46**	−.08	.35
Percentage Fundamentalist	−.51**	−.50**	.35	−.60**
Percentage Catholic	.41*	.50**	−.02	.49**
Socioeconomic Factor	.67**	.76**	−.46**	.71**

**significant at p = .001, *significant at p = .01.

unmarried (.68), and the governor's position on abortion (.46). The Catholic variable is in the positive direction, meaning that in states with large concentrations of Catholics, there tend to be higher abortion rates. Keep in mind that Catholic states also tend to have higher levels of support for abortion in the NES surveys (.49).

Examining correlations with access to abortion, several variables have significant positive correlations with the percentage of counties providing abortions. The number of policy restrictions is negatively correlated with access (−.46), suggesting that states with greater abortion restrictions have fewer abortion providers. States with more pro-choice support (.70), higher socioeconomic levels (.76), greater urban populations (.46), more Catholics (.50), and pro-choice governors (.43) tend to have higher levels of access to abortion. States with larger fundamentalist populations have lower levels of access to abortion (−.50).

Only two variables have strong significant correlations with the nine-point policy measure. The public support measure (−.49) and the socioeconomic variable (−.46) are negatively correlated with the policy index, suggesting that increased levels of these variables produce fewer abortion restrictions in the states.

Reviewing the correlations with the public opinion measure, socioeconomic status of the states (.71), and larger Catholic populations (.49) tend to produce higher levels of support for abortion in the mass public. In contrast, larger numbers of fundamentalist adherents (−.60) tend to lead to lower levels of pro-choice support.

The correlation matrix in table 41 demonstrates the importance of using linear structural equation models (LISREL) with the data. The data set features a large degree of multicollinearity, which can bias and inflate some of the regression estimates. Moreover, severe collinearity violates one of the fundamental assumptions of multiple regression techniques, that no correlation exists among the error terms (Berry and Feldman 1985). LISREL models allow researchers to include the effects of collinearity in their models and still estimate the effects of the variables. Thus, LISREL models bear a truer resemblance to real world data, rather than turning a blind eye to possible bias in the estimates.

A path analysis model was developed using LISREL (Long 1983b; Joreskog and Sorbom 1986). The model features four endogenous variables (abortion rates, access to abortion, abortion policy restrictions, and public support for abortion), and five exogenous variables that model demographic differences among the states (the metropolitan, fundamentalist, Catholic, and socioeconomic factors). The LISREL package allows researchers to estimate the four regression equations simultaneously, based on the observed correlations between all of the variables. Figure 11 presents the standardized regression coefficients from the model.

The model fit statistics suggest that the hypothesized relationships fit the correlations of the variables rather well (Long 1983b; Joreskog and Sorbom 1986). The Chi Square value of 17.8 for 15 degrees of freedom suggests that the model fits the data well. The value for the goodness of fit index (.93) approaches the desired level of 1.0. These fit statistics indicate that the LISREL model produced a covariance matrix much like the original data.

Four variables explain 80 percent of the variance in abortion rates in the American states: the percentage of counties providing abortions, the concentration of metropolitan populations, the policy index, and the percentage of households with unwed residents in the states. Note that the measures of access (percentage of counties) and demand (percentage unmarried) have the strongest positive effect on abortion rates (B = .39), with the percentage of metropolitan population not far behind (B = .25). The policy index has a significant negative effect on abortion rates in the United States, even when controlling for access and demand variables (B = −.21).

When explaining the percentage of counties with abortion providers, two factors come into play. Greater support for abortion in the mass public translates directly into greater levels of access to abortion (B = .32). The only other significant variable to influence the level of providers is the socioeconomic variable (B = .53). The R Square value suggests that 63 percent of the variance in abortion access can be explained using measures of support for abortion and the socioeconomic status of the states. Ironically, the policy variable did not significantly improve the model fit when its path was estimated as influencing abortion access.

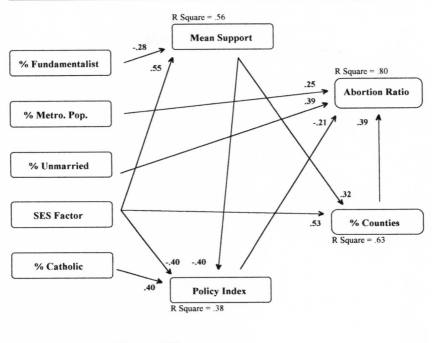

Chi Square with 15 degrees of freedom = 17.80
Root mean square residual = .045
Goodness of Fit Index = .93

Figure 11. A Causal Model of Abortion Ratios in the United States, 1992

The nine-point policy index is parsimoniously explained by three factors: public support for abortion, percentage of Catholics, and socioeconomic levels. Note that greater levels of support for abortion cause fewer abortion policy restrictions (B = −.40), even when controlling for the Catholic and socio-economic variables. The Catholic population variable has a positive effect on the policy measure, indicating that more Catholics in a state tend to produce greater numbers of restrictions (B = .40). Greater levels of socioeconomic status lead to fewer abortion restrictions (B = −.40). These three variables explain 38 percent of the variance in the policy index.

The support for abortion equation should be familiar (it resembles the equation presented in chapter 5). Two variables are significant: the socio-economic variable and the percentage of fundamentalist adherents. The per-centage of fundamentalists has a negative impact on support for abortion (B = −.28). The socioeconomic variable has a strong positive effect on the opinion measure, with higher levels of socioeconomic status (B = .55) producing greater

TABLE 42
A Causal Model of Abortion Rates:
The Direct, Indirect, and Total Effects of Variables

Variable	Direct	Indirect	Total
Socioeconomic Factor		.41	.41
Percentage Counties	.39		.39
Percentage Unmarried	.39		.39
Percentage Metropolitan	.25		.25
Public Support		.21	.21
Policy Index	−.21		−.21
Percentage Catholic		−.08	−.08
Percentage Fundamentalist		−.06	−.06

levels of support for abortion. These two variables account for 56 percent of the variance in the public support factor.

Table 42 lists the direct, indirect, and total effects of the variables on abortion ratios in the states. Overall, the socioeconomic variable has the strongest total influence on abortion rates (.41), all of it indirectly through the influence it has on abortion access, abortion policy, and public support for abortion. The measures of access (percentage of counties) and demand (percentage of unmarried households) have the second strongest impact on abortion rates (.39). The influence of urban populations is seen in the direct effect it can have on abortion rates, even when controlling for other variables (.25). Next come public support for abortion and the measure of policy restrictions, with support for abortion positively influencing abortion rates (.21), and policy restrictions having a negative total effect (−.21). The two religious variables have the weakest influence in the model but have effects in the expected direction. Both the fundamentalist (−.06) and the Catholic variable (−.08) have modest negative influences on state abortion rates.

Conclusion

Although public opinion has been excluded from previous models of the abortion rates in the United States because of methodological problems, this study indicates that it may have a profound impact on abortion utilization through its influence on abortion access and policy. In the same vein that Wright, Erikson, and McIver (1987; Erikson, Wright, and McIver 1993) have argued that state policies reflect state liberalism, abortion use and policy seem to reflect the shape of public opinion within the American states. States in which the public gives more support to keeping abortion open to women tend to have more liberal abortion policies, and more abortion providers are allowed to operate. The result is higher abortion rates.

This is a profound finding, because it provides the link that is expected from democratic theory. In the abortion policy area, mass publics appear to influence policy formation directly, even when we take into account political institutions in the states. Mass preferences get translated into policy, and these policies have influenced the behavior of women seeking abortions. Thus, the link expected from democratic theory between the attitudes of the mass public, policy, and mass behavior can be identified.

Access to abortion, socioeconomic levels, and the urban character of the states remain the most important factors shaping abortion utilization in the American states. An urban rural cleavage appears to be an important variable in explaining state differences in abortion politics. Urban states have more unmarried women and more abortion providers located in large metropolitan centers, allowing women greater access to abortion services. The urban character of the states may also engender more liberalized mass publics, providing a more liberal policy-making environment that might affect access to abortion.

The effects of Catholicism can be seen in the path model. Greater numbers of Catholics do lead to more restrictions on abortion, and thus, have a negative effect on abortion rates. The same can be said for fundamentalist populations: where large concentrations of fundamentalists are located, support for abortion rights is lower. This influence on public support for abortion produces more restrictions on abortion and fewer abortion providers.

8

Conclusion

It is clear that a number of factors converge to shape abortion rates in the American states. A causal model that explains abortion utilization must account for a variety of demographic, religious, political, access, and popular support measures. This concluding chapter summarizes some of the more significant findings presented in this study and offers suggestions for further research.

Struggles over the abortion issue involve fundamental values about when life begins, and issues pertaining to privacy and liberty. Impinging on these issues are religious and moral belief systems that help to shape attitudes toward abortion. Religious denominational variables do not only influence abortion attitudes at the individual level. Research presented here indicates that concentrations of certain religious groups in the American states can influence support for abortion at the aggregate level.

The importance of Catholic, Mormon, and fundamentalist populations for abortion policy-making in the states cannot be denied. Abortion restrictions tend to reach their highest levels in states where fundamentalist cultures predominate. The same can be said for states with large concentrations of Catholics when controlling for other demographic variables. In the chapter detailing policy variation in the states, the percentage of Catholics variable had a significant positive effect on abortion policy restrictions, even when controlling for other variables.

This finding of an important Catholic influence on abortion policy runs counter to earlier findings that states with large Catholic populations tend to be more supportive of abortion rights. With states as the unit of analysis, Catholicism appears to have a pro-choice effect at the level of public opinion; at the policy level, it appears to have an anti-choice effect. Perhaps the two seemingly contradictory findings can be explained in terms of an ambivalent mass public that does not follow church teaching on abortion and reproductive issues on the one hand, and an influential Catholic presence in state legislatures on the other hand. In short, the public opinion finding might simply reflect disagreement with Church positions, while the policy variable reflects slightly better the influence of the Catholic Church in the states.

The influence of Catholic populations must also be placed in the perspective of longitudinal data presented in this study. Massachusetts is an example of a highly Catholic state in which abortion policy was made more restrictive, and abortion utilization dropped to lower levels. This reinforces the finding from the cross-sectional level: states with more Catholics can enact restrictive abortion policies, even though the mass public may not be in line with the policy.

Urbanization and socioeconomic levels continue to play a key role in shaping access to abortion and abortion rates. The wealth and education levels of the states produce varying degrees of support for abortion rights, and varying degrees of policy permissiveness. The measure of metropolitan population is also an important factor in shaping abortion utilization. An urban/rural cleavage has been apparent throughout the era when abortion has been legal in this country. Urban states were first to liberalize their abortion laws and tend to dominate the landscape of abortion clinics. The urban/rural cleavage is bound to grow as abortion providers increasingly disappear from rural states (Henshaw and Van Vort 1994). South and North Dakota now have only one abortion provider within their states (Gorney 1990; Henshaw and Van Vort 1994). Women from rural states seeking abortions face longer travel times, prospects of overnight visits in hotels, and more costly abortions than their urban counterparts (Henshaw and Van Vort 1990).

The Connection of Opinion and Policy

The importance of the strong connection between support for abortion and policy should not be underestimated. Using public support for abortion as a single variable, nearly 25 percent of the variance in policy restrictions can be explained in the states. Few studies in political science turn up such convincing evidence that policy falls in line with mass preferences. A wave of revisionist research is turning to these connections with growing interest, and it is now common to find books and articles that point to a rational public that is in tune with policy (Stimson 1991; Page and Shapiro 1992).

It is also important to highlight the connection between mass publics, policies, and mass behavior expected by democratic theorists. Public opinion is supposed to have some role in shaping public policies. In the rancorous abortion debate that has emerged in the United States, we have lost sight of the fact that state policies closely resemble the policy preferences of the mass publics in the states. Beyond that, policies are enacted to regulate and promote certain modes of behavior. In the abortion realm, policy restrictions have been designed by legislators to do just that—state policymakers either promote the freedom of women to obtain abortion without government interference, or they seek to restrict a mode of behavior that is perceived by many to be immoral. Moreover, state policies either promote equal access to abortion through governmental funding, or they restrict the use of government funds in the interest of promoting childbirth. It seems that these policy approaches have had the expected effect on abortion utilization in the United States. Where mass publics and governments have promoted freedom to choose and equal access to abortion as important values, abortion rates are higher. Where mass publics and governments have promoted the traditional value of childbirth and protecting the potential life of the fetus, abortion rates are lower.

The correlation between opinion and policy becomes more intriguing when examining levels of public support for abortion in the period prior to *Roe v. Wade*. In the 1965 to 1973 era, public approval of abortion in a number of circumstances consistently climbed (Granberg and Granberg 1980; Ebaugh and Haney 1980; Cook, Jelen, and Wilcox 1992; Craig and O'Brien 1993; Garrow 1994). At the same time, states were in the process of enacting new abortion laws that either allowed for more liberal abortion provisions or strengthened restrictions on abortion (Luker 1984). Thus, the liberalization of abortion attitudes in the U.S. appears to have been accompanied by a wave of policy enactments in the United States.

Yet once *Roe* was decided, much of the American public held consistent views on abortion. The analysis presented in chapter 4 suggests that public attitudes on abortion have remained remarkably stable over the past two decades. Thus, policymakers have been operating in an environment of stable majority preferences on the abortion issue.

While aggregate positions on abortion were stable, political institutions that have wrangled with the abortion issue have been unstable. Interest groups representing the extremes of the abortion debate have pressured legislatures and courts to invoke policies that fit their worldview. Shocks to the system, through court decisions or new laws, have forced new tactics upon interest groups on both sides (Goggin 1993; Goggin and Wlezien 1991). Chapter 3 detailed the evolution of the Supreme Court's membership and the impact it had on abortion cases. Political elections have transformed the presidency and Congress into partisan branches periodically at odds with each other over the abortion issue. Between 1973 and 1995, unified control of Congress and the executive branch occurred for only six years, under Presidents Carter and Clinton. Even during the four years of the Carter presidency, federal abortion policy was revamped a number of times to revoke federal funding for most abortions. President Clinton took advantage of his first two years in office to liberalize a number of executive orders pertaining to abortion, including approval of the first trials of the abortion pill, RU-486, in the United States. But the emergence of a Republican majority in Congress is likely to forestall many of his efforts.

In the states, some state legislatures forged new abortion policies that sought to restrict abortion as much as possible under the *Roe* framework. Other state legislatures, recognizing the powder keg that abortion debates can ignite, simply avoided the issue and allowed laws from the late 1800s to remain in their statutes. Still others enacted more permissive laws, or attempted to codify *Roe* into state law (Halva-Neubauer 1990). It seems plausible that some states were in the process of aligning their abortion laws with the perceived mass preferences on abortion issues.

For example, Kentucky abortion laws were revised in 1986 to include use of Medicaid funds only in cases in which a woman's life was in danger, two-parent consent for minors, and a declaration of legislative intent to protect the fetus (NARAL 1989, 37). The law represents one of the most restrictive policies in the Goggin-Kim (1992) index of policy. This is not surprising given the fact that among all fifty states, Kentucky had the lowest level of support for abortion (12 percent) in the NES surveys.

For other states, interest group pressures likely played a greater role in abortion policy change. Yet the measure of interest group strength used in this study did not correlate highly with abortion policies. More research needs to be done to explore abortion interest group strength in the states and its connection with abortion policy. It may be that interest groups respond to policy-making on abortion to a greater extent than they attempt to shape it. Thus, NARAL membership might increase because of perceived efforts to restrict abortion in the states. Likewise, Operation Rescue and pro-life demonstrators who picket outside clinics appear to target states with higher abortion rates.[1]

This is not to say that interest groups do not matter. To a great extent, interest groups have shaped the parameters of the debate over abortion through the rhetoric and arguments they present (Luker 1984; Epstein and Kobylka 1992; Nossiff 1995). Moreover, interest groups have provided a plethora of arguments to the American courts in legal briefs. Indeed, the *Webster* case in 1989 drew a record number of *amici* briefs for a Supreme Court case (Epstein and Kobylka 1992; Craig and O'Brien 1993).

In the end, abortion appears to be an issue that reflects both pluralist notions of democratic theory and majoritarian notions of democracy (Dahl 1960). In one sense, abortion policies in the states reflect aggregate majority preferences. Yet the issue often is staked out by interests and political bodies who feel more intensely about the problem than most Americans. Still, the remarkable finding of this study is the extent to which the majoritarian preferences of the mass public match up with state abortion policies.

---

1. Another measure of interest group activity might be the number of reported clinic protests or acts of violence against clinics that appear in the New York Times. Data culled from the New York Times during the 1985–1989 period suggested such a process was at work—that groups do target states in which access to abortion is great. However, the measure is problematic because the newspaper tends to concentrate its news coverage on more urban states.

The Dilemma of Law and Policy

There is one problem regarding the nine-point policy measure and other policy measures that deserves attention. The assumption is that the aggregation of enacted provisions into state law adequately represents the concept of policy. What if some states are more zealous in upholding their restrictions and laws? What if unconstitutional laws remain in the statute books? Does that deserve to be considered in the policy approach of a state? If some states are more zealous than others in their enforcement of abortion restrictions, then the measure of policy is seriously flawed in some way.

Yet this problem is not damning. If the policies that are not strictly enforced do not qualify as policy, they may qualify as policy intention. The same can be said for unconstitutional laws that are left to remain on the books. They reflect an approach to abortion in the states that signifies a willingness to restrict abortion to a greater extent, or an unwillingness to remove outdated laws from the books. In that sense, unenforced laws represent an approximation to policy that should not be disregarded.

Moreover, any index of abortion policy takes on the quality of a snapshot at one point in time. For example, consider the index of policy restrictions presented by Goggin and Kim (1992) discussed in chapter 6. The measure has no indication of the amount of time or energy devoted to the development of the policies. For example, although North Dakota and Pennsylvania have identical scores on the policy measure (17), one could argue that the development of Pennsylvania's policy picture has been much more hotly contested than North Dakota's. Pennsylvania has been one of the most active states in writing restrictive abortion laws, and pro-life politicians have defended them in two of the most important Supreme Court cases dealing with the issue (*Thornburgh v. American College of Obstetrician and Gynecologists* (1986), and *Planned Parenthood of Southeastern Pennsylvania v. Casey* (1992)).

Despite these shortcomings, the policy measure does appear to be a good surrogate of abortion policy in the states. It is likely that the ranking of states on the index would satisfy most scholars as an appropriate listing of the variation in state approaches to abortion.

Future Research

This book ends much in the way it began: with a call for more systematic research on abortion politics. Echoing Malcolm Goggin's (1993) plea, there is much to be done in the field to enhance our understanding of the politics of abortion.

Time series analysis must be brought to bear on a number of questions dealing with abortion. Examples presented in this study suggest that the impact of policy change is best modeled at the state level. When examining the effects of national policy changes (*Roe v. Wade*, the Hyde Amendment, the Reagan-Bush era, and *Webster*), no significant impacts were found. These findings will no doubt be better received when the series of data lengthens through more observations.

What is needed at the state level are more studies that apply interrupted time series models to abortion policy changes (Korenbrot et al. 1986). Abortion rate time series for all fifty states cry out for comparison. For example, states with parental notification provisions can be compared with a group of states that lack such a provision. Comparisons improve the validity of findings when effects after the intervention fail to show up in other similar states. With Supreme Court rulings in *Webster* and *Casey* in 1989 and 1992 having opened the field of abortion regulation to the states even more, time series models that test the impact of these rulings will become testable in the future.

Abortion researchers also need to focus more on the "residuals," or outlier states, that do not fit general tendencies (Norrander and Wilcox 1993). We do not do a very good job accounting for states like West Virginia, where support for abortion is low in the mass public, yet few abortion policy restrictions exist: despite permissive abortion policies, abortion rates are low. Undoubtedly, the main explanatory variable here is the rural character of much of the state. But detailed case studies of interesting states can tackle this gap in the research. Glen Halva-Neubauer (1992, 1995) has done such an analysis of abortion politics in Minnesota. Moreover, a recent book on abortion politics in ten of the states has made a significant contribution to this line of inquiry (Segers and Byrnes 1995). Several essays in that collection help explain why liberal policies have emerged in states that are normally considered conservative (O'Neill 1995; Strickland 1995), and conservative policies have been enacted in states generally seen as liberal (Halva-Neubauer 1995).

Perhaps most important for future research is the need for more analysis of aggregate public opinion variables and their relationship with abortion policy and abortion rates. Having a new source of data available on abortion attitudes should inspire a number of new research efforts. In the spirit of Wright, Erikson, and McIver (1987; Erikson, Wright, and McIver 1993), we need to better explain how state preferences on abortion issues impact abortion politics. In the end, our pursuit is likely to demonstrate the wisdom of V. O. Key (1961, 7) when he said that public opinion must influence policies or else "all the talk about democracy is nonsense."

References

Ada v. Guam Society of Obstetricians and Gynecologists. 113 Sup. Ct. 633 (1993).

Akron v. Akron Center for Reproductive Health. 462 U.S. 416 (1983).

Albritton, Robert B. 1990. Social services: Welfare and health. In *Politics in the American states*, 5th ed. Virginia Gray, Herbert Jacob, and Robert B. Albritton, eds. Glenview, Ill.: Scott, Foresman and Company.

Albritton, Robert B., and Matthew E. Wetstein. 1991. "The Determinants of Abortion Use in the American States." Paper presented at the annual meeting of the Midwest Political Science Association, Chicago.

Arney, William R., and William H. Trescher. 1976. Trends in attitudes toward abortion, 1972–1975. *Family Planning Perspectives* 8: 117–124.

Asher, Herbert B. 1983. *Causal modeling.* Sage University Paper Series on Quantitative Applications in the Social Sciences, series no. 07–003. Newbury Park, Calif.: Sage Publications.

Baker, Ross, Laurily Epstein, and Rodney Forth. 1981. Matters of life and death: Social, political, and religious correlates of attitudes on abortion. *American Politics Quarterly* 9: 89–102.

Barone, Michael and Grant Ujifusa. 1989. *The Almanac of American Politics 1990.* Washington, D.C.: The National Journal.

Baum, Lawrence. 1989. *The Supreme Court.* Washington, D.C.: CQ Press.

Beal v. Doe. 432 U.S. 438 (1977).

Bellotti v. Baird. 443 U.S. 622 (1979).

Benson, Peter, and Dorothy Williams. 1982. *Religion on Capitol Hill.* San Francisco: Harper & Row.

Berkman, Michael B., and Robert O'Connor. 1992. "The Determinants of State Abortion Policies: A Post–Webster Analysis." Paper presented at the annual meeting of the Midwest Political Science Association, Chicago, Ill.

———. 1993. Do women legislators matter? Female legislators and state abortion policy. *American Politics Quarterly* 21: 102–124. Also in *Understanding the New Politics of Abortion*, Malcolm Goggin, ed. Newbury Park, Calif.: Sage Publications, 268–283.

Berry, William D., and Stanley Feldman. 1985. *Multiple regression in practice*. Sage University Paper Series on Quantitative Applications in the Social Sciences, series no. 07–050. Newbury Park, Calif.: Sage Publications.

Bishop, George F., Robert W. Oldendick, and Alfred J. Tuchfarber. 1985. The importance of replicating a failure to replicate: Order effects on abortion items. *Public Opinion Quarterly* 49: 105–114.

Blank, Robert H. 1984. Judicial decision making and biological fact: *Roe v. Wade* and the unresolved question of fetal viability. *Western Political Quarterly* 37: 584–602.

Borrelli, MaryAnne. 1995. Massachusetts: Abortion policymaking in transition. In *Abortion Politics in American States*, Mary C. Segers and Timothy A. Byrnes, eds. Armonk, N.Y.: M. E. Sharpe, 183–204.

Box, George E. P., and Gwilym M. Jenkins. 1976. *Time Series Analysis: Forecasting and Control*, revised ed. Oakland, Calif.: Holden-Day.

Bray v. Alexandria Women's Health Clinic. 113 Sup. Ct. 753 (1993).

Buchanan, James M., and Gordon Tullock. 1962. *The Calculus of Consent: Logical Foundations of Constitutional Democracy*. Ann Arbor: University of Michigan Press.

Byrnes, Timothy A., and Mary C. Segers, eds. 1992. *The Catholic Church and the Politics of Abortion: A View from the States*. Boulder, Colo.: Westview Press.

Campbell, Angus, Philip E. Converse, Warren E. Miller, and Donald E. Stokes. 1960. *The American Voter*. New York: John Wiley and Sons.

Campbell, Donald T., and Julian C. Stanley. 1966. *Experimental and Quasiexperimental Designs for Research*. Chicago: Rand McNally.

Canon, Bradley C. 1992. The Supreme Court as a cheerleader in politico–moral disputes. *Journal of Politics* 54: 637–653.

Carmines, Edward G., and James A. Stimson. 1980. The two faces of issue voting. *American Political Science Review* 74: 78–91.

Cartoof, Virginia G., and Lorraine V. Klerman. 1986. Parental consent for abortion: Impact of the Massachusetts law. *American Journal of Public Health* 76 (No. 4): 397–400.

Center for Governmental Studies, Northern Illinois University. 1989–1992. *Codebook for the Illinois Policy Survey*. DeKalb, Ill.: Center for Governmental Studies, Northern Illinois University.

Center for Political Studies. various years. *National Election Series Panel Studies*, 1972–76, 1988–1990–1992. Machine readable data files and codebooks. Center for Political Studies, Institute for Social Research, University of Michigan, Ann Arbor, Mich.

Cigler, Allan J., and Burdette A. Loomis, eds. 1986. *Interest Group Politics*, 2nd ed. Washington, D.C.: Congressional Quarterly Press.

Colautti v. Franklin. 439 U.S. 379 (1979).

Combs, Michael W., and Susan Welch. 1982. Blacks, whites, and attitudes toward abortion. *Public Opinion Quarterly* 46: 510–520.

Committee to Defend Reproductive Rights v. Myers. Cal., 625 P.2d. 779 (1981).

Converse, Philip E. 1964. The nature of belief systems in mass publics. In *Ideology and Discontent*, David E. Apter, ed. Glencoe, Ill.: Free Press.

Converse, Philip E., and Gregory B. Markus. 1979. *Plus ca change...*: The new CPS election study panel. *American Political Science Review* 73: 32–49.

Cook, Thomas D., and Donald T. Campbell. 1979. *Quasi–experimentation: Design and Analysis Issues for Field Settings.* Boston: Houghton Mifflin.

Cook, Elizabeth Adell, Ted G. Jelen, and Clyde Wilcox. 1991. "Generations and Abortion." Paper presented at the annual meeting of the Midwest Political Science Association, Chicago, Ill.

―――. 1992. *Between Two Absolutes: Public Opinion and the Politics of Abortion.* Boulder, Colo.: Westview Press.

Craig, Barbara, and David M. O'Brien. 1993. *Abortion and American Politics.* Chatham, N.J.: Chatham House Publishers.

Dahl, Robert A. 1956. *A preface to Democratic Theory.* Chicago: University of Chicago Press.

Darcy, R., Susan Welch, and Janet Clark. 1987. *Women, Elections and Representation.* New York: Longman.

Davis, James A., and Tom W. Smith. 1990. *General Social Surveys, 1972–1989.* Codebook and machine–readable data files. Chicago: National Opinion Research Center.

Day, Christine L. 1992. "State Legislative Voting Patterns on Abortion in Louisiana Since the *Webster* Decision." Paper presented at the annual meeting of the Midwest Political Science Association, Chicago, Ill.

Daynes, Byron W., and Raymond Tatalovich. 1984. Religious influence and congressional voting on abortion. *Journal for the Scientific Study of Religion* 23: 197–200.

Dodson, Debra L., and Lauren D. Burnbauer. 1990. *Election 1989: The Abortion Issue in New Jersey and Virginia.* New Brunswick, N.J.: Eagleton Institute of Politics.

Doe v. Bolton. 410 U.S. 179 (1973).

Downs, Anthony. 1957. *An Economic Theory of Democracy.* New York: Harper.

Dran, Ellen M. 1993. Personal communication, April 13, 1993.

Ducat, Craig R. and Harold W. Chase. 1992a. *Constitutional Interpretation*, 5th ed. St. Paul, Minn.: West Publishing Company.

————. 1992b. *1992 Supplement to constitutional interpretation*, fifth edition. St. Paul, Minn.: West Publishing Company.

Ducat, Craig R., and Robert Dudley. 1987. Dimensions underlying economic policy making in the early and late Burger Courts. *Journal of Politics* 49: 521–539.

Ebaugh, Helen Rose Fuchs, and C. Allan Haney. 1980. Shifts in abortion attitudes: 1972–1982. *Journal of Marriage and the Family* 42: 491–499.

Eccles, Mary E. 1978. Abortion: How members voted in 1977. *Congressional Quarterly Weekly Report* 36: 258–267.

Elazar, Daniel. 1984. *American Federalism: A View from the States*, 3rd ed. New York: Harper and Row.

Epstein, Lee and Joseph F. Kobylka. 1992. *The Supreme Court and Legal Change: Abortion and the Death Penalty*. Chapel Hill, N.C.: University of North Carolina Press.

Erikson, Robert S., Gerald C. Wright, and John P. McIver. 1993. *Statehouse Democracy: Public Opinion and Policy in the American States*. Cambridge: Cambridge University Press.

Ezzard, Nancy V., Willard Cates, Jr., Dorine G. Kramer, and Christopher Tietze. 1982. Race–specific patterns of abortion use by American teenagers. *American Journal of Public Health* 72 (No. 8): 809–814.

Fiorina, Morris. 1981. *Retrospective Voting in American National Elections*. New Haven: Yale University Press.

Franklin, Charles H., and Liane Kosacki. 1989. Republican schoolmaster: The U.S. Supreme Court, public opinion, and abortion. *American Political Science Review* 83: 751–771.

Gais, Thomas L., Mark A. Peterson, and Jack Walker. 1984. Interest groups, iron triangles, and representative institutions in American national government. *British Journal of Political Science* 14: 161–185.

Gallup, George, Jr., and Frank Newport. 1990. Americans shift toward pro–choice position. *The Gallup Poll Monthly* No. 295: 2–4.

Gallup Report. 1989. Majority critical of abortion decision, but most Americans favor some new restrictions. *Gallup Report* No. 286: 5–11.

Garrow, David J. 1994. *Liberty and Sexuality: The Right to Privacy and the Making of Roe v. Wade*. New York: Macmillan.

Glass, Gene V., Victor L. Willson, and John M. Gottman. 1975. *Design and Analysis of Time Series Experiments*. Boulder, Colo.: Colorado Associated University Press.

Glazer, Sarah. 1987. Abortion policy. *Editorial Research Reports*, October 16, 1987: 534–547.

Goggin, Malcolm L. 1992. "The Tactical Choices of Abortion Interest Groups." Paper presented at the annual meeting of the Midwest Political Science Association, Chicago, Ill.

———. 1993. Understanding the new politics of abortion: A framework and agenda for research. *American Politics Quarterly* 21: 4–30.

Goggin, Malcolm L., and Jung–Ki Kim. 1992. "Interest Groups, Public Opinion, and Abortion Policy in the American States." Paper presented at the 1992 annual meeting of the Western Political Science Association, San Francisco, Calif.

Goggin, Malcolm L., and Christopher Wlezien. 1991. "Interest Groups and The Socialization of Conflict." Paper presented at the annual meeting of the Midwest Political Science Association.

———, and Christopher Wlezien. 1993. Abortion opinion and policy in the American states. In *Understanding the New Politics of Abortion*, Malcolm Goggin, ed. Newbury Park, Calif.: Sage Publications, 190–202.

Gold, Edwin M., Carl L. Erhardt, Harold Jacobziner, and Frieda G. Nelson. 1965. Therapeutic abortions in New York City: A 20–year review. *American Journal of Public Health* 55 (No. 7): 964–972.

Gorney, Cynthia. 1990. Getting an abortion in the heartland: For pro–choice women in South Dakota, there's only one choice. *Washington Post National Weekly Edition*, October 15, 1990: 10–11.

Granberg, Donald M., and Beth Wellman Granberg. 1980. Abortion attitudes, 1965–1980: Trends and determinants. *Family Planning Perspectives* 12: 250–261.

Gray, Virginia, Herbert Jacob, and Robert B. Albritton, eds. 1990. *Politics in the American States*, 5th ed. Glenview, Ill.: Scott, Foresman and Company.

Griswold v. Connecticut. 391 U.S. 145 (1965).

Guth, James, and Glen Halva–Neubauer. 1993. "Abortion Access in the States: The Impact of Public Opinion and Religion." Paper presented at the annual meeting of the Midwest Political Science Association, Chicago.

H. L. v. Matheson. 450 U.S. 398 (1981).

Haas–Wilson, Deborah. 1993. The economic impact of state restrictions on abortion: Parental consent and notification laws and Medicaid funding restrictions. *Journal of Policy Analysis and Management* 12: 498–511.

Hall, Elaine J., and Myra Marx Ferree. 1986. Race differences in abortion attitudes. *Public Opinion Quarterly* 50: 193–207.

Halva–Neubauer, Glen. 1989. "The Reversal of *Roe*: A View from the States." Paper presented at the annual meeting of the American Political Science Association, Atlanta.

———. 1990. Abortion policy in the post–*Webster* age. *Publius: The Journal of Federalism* 20: 27–44.

————. 1992. Legislative agenda setting in the states: The case of abortion policy. Ph.D. dissertation, University of Minnesota.

————. 1995. Minnesota: Shifting Sands on a "Challenger" Beachhead. In *Abortion Politics in American States*, Mary C. Segers and Timothy A. Byrnes, eds. Armonk, N.Y.: M. E. Sharpe, 29–50.

Hansen, Susan B. 1980. State implementation of Supreme Court decisions: Abortion rates since *Roe v. Wade. Journal of Politics* 42: 372–395.

————. 1993. Differences in public policies toward abortion: The electoral and policy context. In *Understanding the New Politics of Abortion*, Malcolm Goggin, ed. Newbury Park, Calif.: Sage Publications, 222–248.

Harris v. McRae. 448 U.S. 297 (1980).

Henry, Norah H., and Milton E. Harvey. 1982. Social, spatial and political determinants of U.S. abortion rates. *Social Science Medicine* 16: 987–996.

Henshaw, Stanley K. 1991. The accessibility of abortion services in the United States. *Family Planning Perspectives* 23: 246–252.

Henshaw, Stanley K., Lisa M. Koonin, and Jack C. Smith. 1991. Characteristics of U.S. women having abortions, 1987. *Family Planning Perspectives* 23: 75–82.

Henshaw, Stanley K., and Jennifer Van Vort, eds. 1988. *Abortion Services in the United States, Each State, and Metropolitan Area, 1984–1985*. New York: The Alan Guttmacher Institute.

————. 1990. Abortion services in the United States, 1987 and 1988. Family Planning Perspectives 22: 102–108.

————. 1994. Abortion services in the United States, 1991 and 1992. *Family Planning Perspectives* 26: 100–106, 112.

Hertel, Bradley R., and Michael Hughes. 1987. Religious affiliation, attendance, and support for pro–family issues in the United States. *Social Forces* 65: 858–882.

Hodgson v. Minnesota. 497 U.S. 417 (1990).

Jackson, Robert A. 1992. Effects of public opinion and political system characteristics on state policy outcomes. *Publius: The Journal of Federalism*, 22 (1992): 31–46.

Jacobs, Lawrence R. 1992a. Institutions and culture: Health policy and public opinion in the United States and Britain. *World Politics* 44: 179–209.

————. 1992b. The recoil effect: Public opinion and policy making in the United States and Britain. *Comparative Politics* 24: 199–217.

————. 1993. *The Health of Nations: Public Opinion and the Making of American and British Health Policy*. Ithaca, N.Y.: Cornell University Press.

Jelen, Ted G. 1988. Changes in the attitudinal correlations of abortion, 1977–1985. *Journal for the Scientific Study of Religion* 27: 211–228.

Johnson, Charles A., and Jon R. Bond. 1982. Policy implementation and responsiveness in nongovernmental institutions: Hospital abortion services after *Roe v. Wade. Western Political Quarterly* 35: 385–405.

Johnson, Charles A., and Bradley C. Canon. 1984. *Judicial policies: Implementation and impact.* Washington, D.C.: Congressional Quarterly Inc.

Joreskog, Karl G., and Dag Sorbom. 1986. *LISREL VI: User's guide.* Chicago, Ill.: National Educational Resources.

Judd, Charles, and D. Kenny. 1981. The interrupted time series design. In *Estimating the Effects of Social Interventions.* Cambridge, Mass.: Harvard University Press.

Kathlene, Lyn. 1992. "Power and Influence in State Legislative Policymaking: The Interaction of Gender and Position in Committee Hearing Debates." Paper presented at the annual meeting of the American Political Science Association, Chicago, Ill.

Key, V. O. 1961. *Public Opinion and American Democracy.* New York: Knopf.

Kim, Jae-On, and Charles W. Mueller. 1978. *Introduction to Factor Analysis.* Sage University Series on Quantitative Applications in the Social Sciences, series no. 07–013. Newbury Park, Calif.: Sage Publications.

Kinder, Donald R. 1983. Diversity and complexity in American public opinion. In *Political Science: The State of the Discipline*, Ada Finifter, ed. Washington, D.C.: American Political Science Association.

Korenbrot, Carol C., Claire Brindis, and Fran Priddy. 1990. Trends in rates of live births and abortions following state restrictions on public funding of abortion. *Public Health Reports* 105 (No. 6): 555–562.

Kosmin, Barry A., and Seymour P. Lachman. 1991. Research Report: The National Survey of Religious Identification, 1989–1990 (selected tabulations). New York: The Graduate School and University Center of the City University of New York.

Krosnick, Jon A. 1991. The stability of political preferences: Comparisons of symbolic and nonsymbolic attitudes. *American Journal of Political Science* 35: 547–576.

Legge, Jerome S., Jr. 1983. The determinants of attitudes toward abortion in the American electorate. *Western Political Quarterly* 36: 479–490.

———. 1985. *Abortion Policy: An Evaluation of the Consequences for Maternal and Infant Health.* Albany, N.Y.: State University of New York Press.

Long, J. Scott. 1983a. *Confirmatory Factor Analysis.* Sage University Paper Series on Quantitative Applications in the Social Sciences, series no. 07–033. Newbury Park, Calif.: Sage Publications.

————. 1983b. *Covariance Structural Models*. Sage University Paper Series on Quantitative Applications in the Social Sciences, series no. 07–034. Newbury Park, Calif.: Sage Publications.

Lowi, Theodore J. 1969. *The End of Liberalism: Ideology, Policy, and the Crisis of Public Authority*. New York: Norton.

Luker, Kristin. 1984. *Abortion and the Politics of Motherhood*. Berkeley, Calif.: University of California Press.

Luttbeg, Norman R. 1992. *Comparing the States and Communities: Politics, Government, and Policy in the United States*. New York: HarperCollins Publishers.

Madsen v. Woman's Health Center. 114 Sup. Ct. 2516 (1994).

Maher v. Roe. 432 U.S. 464 (1977).

Manheim, Jarol B., and Richard C. Rich. 1986. *Empirical Political Analysis: Research Methods in Political Science*. New York: Longman Inc.

McCleary, Richard, and Richard A. Hay, Jr. 1980. *Applied Time Series Analysis for the Social Sciences*. Newbury Park, Calif.: Sage Publications.

McConnell, Grant. 1966. *Private Power and American Democracy*. New York: Knopf.

McDowall, David, Richard McCleary, Errol E. Meidinger, and Richard A. Hay, Jr. 1980. *Interrupted time series analysis*. Sage University Paper Series on Quantitative Applications in the Social Sciences, series no. 07–021. Newbury Park, Calif.: Sage Publications.

Medoff, Marshall H. 1988. An economic analysis of the demand for abortions. *Economic Inquiry* 26: 353–359.

Meier, Kenneth J., and Deborah R. McFarlane. 1992. State policies on funding of abortions: A pooled time series analysis. *Social Science Quarterly* 73: 690–698.

————. 1993. The politics of funding abortion: State responses to the political environment. *American Politics Quarterly* 21: 81–101.

Mezey, Susan Gluck. 1992. *In Pursuit of Equality: Women, Public Policy, and the Federal Courts*. New York: St. Martin's Press.

Mileti, Dennis S., and Larry D. Barnett. 1972. Nine demographic factors and their relationship to attitudes toward abortion legalization. *Social Biology* 19: 43–50.

Mills, C. Wright. 1956. *The Power Elite*. New York: Oxford University Press.

National Abortion Rights Action League (NARAL). 1989. *Who Decides? A State by State Review of Abortion Rights in America*. Washington, D.C.: NARAL/The NARAL Foundation.

————. 1992. *Who Decides? A State by State Review of Abortion Rights*, 3rd ed. Washington, D.C.: NARAL/The NARAL Foundation.

National Opinion Research Center. various years. *General Social Survey.* Machine readable data files and codebooks. Chicago: National Opinion Research Center, University of Chicago.

National Organization for Women v. Scheidler. 114 Sup. Ct. 798 (1994).

New York Times v. Sullivan. 376 U.S. 254 (1964).

Nie, Norman H., Sidney Verba and John R. Petrocik. 1979. *The Changing American Voter.* Cambridge: Harvard University Press.

Norrander, Barbara, and Clyde Wilcox. 1993. "The Sources of State Abortion Policy." Paper presented at the annual meeting of the Midwest Political Science Association, Chicago.

Nossiff, Rosemary. 1995. Pennsylvania: The Impact of Party Organization and Religions Lobbying. In *Abortion Politics in American States*, Mary C. Segers and Timothy A. Byrnes, eds. Armonk, N.Y.: M. E. Sharpe, 16–28.

O'Brien, David. 1986. *Storm Center: The Supreme Court in American Politics.* New York: W. W. Norton and Company

Ohio v. Akron Center for Reproductive Health. 497 U.S. 502 (1990).

O'Neill, Daniel J. 1995. Arizona: Pro-Choice Success in a Conservative, Republican State. In *Abortion Politics in American States*, Mary C. Segers and Timothy A. Byrnes, eds. Armonk, N.Y.: M. E. Sharpe, 84–101.

Ostrom, Charles W., Jr. 1978. *Time Series Analysis: Regression Techniques.* Sage University Paper Series on Quantitative Applications in the Social Sciences, series no. 07–009. Newbury Park, Calif.: Sage Publications.

Page, Benjamin I., and Robert Y. Shapiro. 1983. Effects of public opinion on policy. *American Political Science Review* 77: 175–190.

———. 1992. *The Rational Public.* Chicago: University of Chicago Press.

Peltzman, Sam. 1984. Constituent interests and congressional voting. *Journal of Law and Economics* 27: 181–210.

Petchesky, Rosalind. 1984. *Abortion and Woman's Choice: The State, Sexuality, and Reproductive Freedom.* New York: Longman Publishers.

Planned Parenthood Association of Kansas City v. Ashcroft. 462 U.S. 476 (1983).

Planned Parenthood of Central Missouri v. Danforth. 428 U.S. 52 (1976).

Planned Parenthood of Southeastern Pennsylvania v. Casey. 112 Sup. Ct. 2791 (1992).

Poelker v. Doe. 432 U.S. 519 (1977).

Powell-Griner, Eve, and Katherine Trent. 1987. The sociodemographic determinants of abortion in the United States. *Demography* 24: 553–561.

Quinn, Bernard, Herman Anderson, Martin Bradley, Paul Goetting, and Peggy Shriver. 1982. *Churches and Church Membership in the United States, 1980*. Atlanta: Glenmary Research Center.

Renzi, Mario. 1975. Ideal family size as an intervening variable between religion and attitudes towards abortion. *Journal for the Scientific Study of Religion* 14: 23–27.

Richard, Patricia Bayer. 1995. Ohio: Steering toward Middle Ground. In *Abortion Politics in American States*, Mary C. Segers and Timothy A. Byrnes, eds. Armonk, N.Y.: M. E. Sharpe, 127–151.

Roe v. Wade. 410 U.S. 113 (1973).

Rogers, James L., Robert F. Boruch, George B. Stoms, and Dorothy DeMoya. 1991. Impact of the Minnesota parental notification law on abortion and birth. *American Journal of Public Health* 81 (No. 3): 294–298.

Rohde, David, and Harold Spaeth. 1976. *Supreme Court Decision Making*. San Francisco: W. H. Freeman.

Rosenberg, Gerald N. 1991. *The Hollow Hope: Can Courts Bring About Social Change?* Chicago, Ill.: University of Chicago Press.

Rosenblatt, Roger. 1992. *Life Itself: Abortion in the American Mind*. New York: Random House.

Rossi, Alice S., and Bhavani Sitaraman. 1988. Abortion in Context: Historical Trends and Future Changes. *Family Planning Perspectives* 20: 273–281.

Russo, Michael. 1995. California: A Political Landscape for Choice and Conflict. In *Abortion Politics in American States*, Mary C. Segers and Timothy A. Byrnes, eds. Armonk, NY: M. E. Sharpe, 168–181.

Rust v. Sullivan. 111 Sup. Ct. 1759 (1991).

Schaefer, George, editor. 1971. "Legal Abortions in New York State: Medical, Legal, Nursing, Social Aspects." A symposium of essays originally published in *Clinical Obstetrics and Gynecology*, 14 (No. 1). New York: Harper & Row Publishers.

Schattschneider, E. E. 1960. *The Semisovereign People*. New York: Holt, Rinehart and Winston.

Schlozman, Kay Lehman, and John T. Tierney. 1986. *Organized Interests in American Democracy*. New York: Harper and Row.

Schnell, Frauke. 1991. "The Abortion Issue: Value Conflict and Attitude Strength." Paper presented at the annual meeting of the Midwest Political Science Association, Chicago, Ill.

———. 1993. The foundations of abortion attitudes: The role of values and value conflict. In *Understanding the New Politics of Abortion*, Malcolm Goggin, ed. Newbury Park, Calif.: Sage Publications, 23–43.

Schubert, Glendon. 1963. Civilian control and stare decisis in the Warren Court. In *Judicial Decision–Making*, Glendon Schubert, ed. New York: The Free Press of Glencoe, 55–77.

Segal, Jeffrey. 1987. Senate confirmation of Supreme Court justices: Partisan and institutional politics. *Journal of Politics* 49: 998–1010.

Segal, Jeffrey, and Harold Spaeth. 1993. *The Supreme Court and the Attitudinal Model.* Cambridge: Cambridge University Press.

Segers, Mary C., and Timothy A. Byrnes, eds. 1995. *Abortion Politics in American States.* Armonk, N.Y.: M. E. Sharpe.

Simonopoulos v. Virginia. 462 U.S. 506 (1983).

Smith v. Bentley. 493 F. Supp. 916, E. D. Ark. (1980).

Smith, Eric R. A. N. 1989. *The Unchanging American Voter.* Berkeley, Calif.: University of California Press.

Spaeth, Harold J. 1963. Warren court attitudes toward business: The "B" scale. In *Judicial decision–making*, Glendon Schubert, ed. New York: The Free Press of Glencoe, 79–108.

Staggenborg, Suzanne. 1991. *The pro–choice movement: Organization and activism in the abortion conflict.* New York: Oxford University Press.

Stimson, James A. 1991. *Public Opinion in America: Moods, Cycles and Swings.* Boulder, Colo.: Westview Press.

Strickland, Ruth Ann. 1995. North Carolina: One Liberal Law in the South. In *Abortion Politics in American States*, Mary C. Segers and Timothy A. Byrnes, eds. Armonk, N.Y.: M. E. Sharpe, 102–126.

Sullivan, Kathleen M. 1994. Law's labors. *New Republic* May 23, 1994, 42–46.

Tatalovich, Raymond A., and Byron W. Daynes. 1981. *The politics of abortion.* New York: Praeger Publishers.

———. 1989. The geographic distribution of U.S. hospitals with abortion facilities. *Family Planning Perspectives* 21: 81–84.

Tatalovich, Raymond, and David Schier. 1993. The persistence of ideological cleavage in voting on abortion legislation in the House of Representatives, 1973–1988. *American Politics Quarterly* 21: 125–139. Also in *Understanding the New Politics of Abortion*, Malcolm Goggin, ed. Newbury Park, Calif.: Sage Publications, 109–122.

Tedrow, Lucky M., and E. R. Mahoney. 1979. Trends in attitudes toward abortion: 1972–1976. *Public Opinion Quarterly* 43: 181–189.

Thomas, Susan. 1991. The impact of women on state legislative policies. *Journal of Politics* 53: 958–976.

Thomas, Susan, and Susan Welch. 1991. The impact of gender on activities and priorities of state legislators. *Western Political Quarterly* 44: 445–456.

Thornburgh v. American College of Obstetricians and Gynecologists. 476 U.S. 747 (1986).

Trager, Oliver, ed. 1993. *Abortion: Choice and Conflict.* New York: Facts on File, Inc.

Tribe, Laurence. 1991. *Abortion: The Clash of Absolutes.* New York: Norton.

U.S. Census Bureau. various years. *Statistical Abstract of the United States.* Washington, D.C.: U.S. Government Printing Office.

U.S. Centers for Disease Control. various years. *Abortion Surveillance.* Washington, D.C.: U.S. Department of Health Education and Welfare (Health and Human Services), Public Health Service.

———. 1976. *Morbidity and Mortality Weekly Report* 24 (No. 54). Washington, D.C.: U.S. Government Printing Office.

———. 1977. *Morbidity and Mortality Weekly Report* 25 (No. 53). Washington, D.C.: U.S. Government Printing Office.

———. 1978. *Morbidity and Mortality Weekly Report* 26 (No. 53). Washington, D.C.: U.S. Government Printing Office.

———. 1979. *Morbidity and Mortality Weekly Report* 27 (No. 54). Washington, D.C.: U.S. Government Printing Office.

———. 1980. *Morbidity and Mortality Weekly Report* 28 (No. 54). Washington, D.C.: U.S. Government Printing Office.

———. 1981. *Morbidity and Mortality Weekly Report* 29 (No. 54). Washington, D.C.: U.S. Government Printing Office.

———. 1983. *Morbidity and Mortality Weekly Report* 31 (No. 54). Washington, D.C.: U.S. Government Printing Office.

———. 1984. *Morbidity and Mortality Weekly Report* 33 (No. 3SS). Washington, D.C.: U.S. Government Printing Office.

———. 1987. *Morbidity and Mortality Weekly Report* 36 (No. 1SS). Washington, D.C.: U.S. Government Printing Office.

———. 1989. *Morbidity and Mortality Weekly Report* 38 (No. 2SS). Washington, D.C.: U.S. Government Printing Office.

———. 1990. *Morbidity and Mortality Weekly Report* 39 (No. 2SS). Washington, D.C.: U.S. Government Printing Office.

———. 1991. *Morbidity and Mortality Weekly Report* 40 (No. 1SS). Washington, D.C.: U.S. Government Printing Office.

————. 1992. *Morbidity and Mortality Weekly Report* 41 (No. 2SS). Washington, D.C.: U.S. Government Printing Office.

U.S. National Center for Health Statistics. various years. *Health, United States*. Washington, D.C.: Public Health Service.

Vinovskis, Maris. 1980. The politics of abortion in the House of Representatives in 1976. In *The Law and Politics of Abortion*, Carl E. Schneider and Maris Vinovskis, eds. Lexington, Mass.: Lexington Books.

Weber, Ronald E., and William R. Shaffer. 1972. Public opinion and American state policy making. *Midwest Journal of Political Science* 16: 633–699.

Weber, Ronald E., Ann H. Hopkins, Michael L. Mexey, and Frank Munger. 1972. Computer simulation of state electorates. *Public Opinion Quarterly* 36: 49–65.

Webster v. Reproductive Health Services. 492 U.S. 490 (1989).

Weiner, Janet, and Barbara A. Bernhardt. 1990. A survey of state Medicaid policies for coverage of abortion and prenatal diagnostic procedures. *American Journal of Public Health* 80: 717–720.

Wetstein, Matthew. 1993. A LISREL model of public opinion on abortion. In *Understanding the new politics of abortion*, Malcolm Goggin, ed. Newbury Park, Calif.: Sage Publications, 57–70.

Wetstein, Matthew, and Cynthia Ostberg. 1993. "Senate Voting on Abortion: A New Look at the Dimensionality Controversy." Paper presented at the annual meeting of the Southwest Political Science Association, New Orleans.

Wilcox, Clyde. 1990. Race differences and abortion attitudes: Some additional evidence. *Public Opinion Quarterly* 54: 248–255.

————. 1992. Race, religion, region and abortion attitudes. *Sociological Analysis* 53: 97–105.

Witt, Stephanie L., and Gary Moncrief. 1993. Religion and roll call voting in Idaho: the 1990 abortion controversy. *American Politics Quarterly* 21: 140–149. Also in *Understanding the New Politics of Abortion*, Malcolm Goggin, ed. Newbury Park, Calif.: Sage Publications, 123–133.

Woliver, Laura R. 1991. "Mobilizing the Pro–Choice Movement in South Carolina." Paper presented at the annual meeting of the Midwest Political Science Association, Chicago, IL.

Wright, Gerald C., Jr., Robert S. Erikson, and John P. McIver. 1987. Public opinion and policy liberalism in the American states. *American Journal of Political Science* 31: 980–1001.

————. 1985. Measuring state partisanship and ideology with survey data. *Journal of Politics* 47: 469–489.

Zbaraz v. Hartigan. 484 U.S. 171 (1987).

Index

Pennsylvania
  abortion policy, 86, 95
  abortion rates, 52–54
  medicaid policy, 19, 52–54
  policy change after *Webster*, 23–24
  spousal notification provision, 24
Petchesky, Rosalind, 2
Peterson, Mark, 3
Petrocik, John, 65
*Planned Parenthood Association of
  Kansas City v. Ashcroft*, 17, 21, 29,
  34–35
*Planned Parenthood of Central Missouri
  v. Danforth*, 15–17, 21, 28, 32–33
*Planned Parenthood of Southeastern
  Pennsylvania v. Casey*, 23–25, 27, 30,
  34, 36, 57, 73, 95, 129–30
pluralist approach to policy making, 3–4,
  128
Poelker v. Doe, 19–20, 21, 28, 32–33, 34
policy liberalism, 92
policy mood, 5, 45
political culture, 77, 104, 105–109
political parties
  mediating role of, 4
  identification with, 66–67
  ratio of Democrats to Republicans, 102,
    105–9, 115
Powell–Griner, Eve, 68, 116
Powell, Justice Lewis, 17–18
  voting behavior in abortion cases,
    28–35, 38–39
premarital sex, attitudes on 68–72
principal components analysis (factor
  analysis), 69–70, 98–99
pro–choice groups, 8, 104
Pro–Life Action Network (PLAN), 26
pro–life groups, 8, 26, 128
Protestants
  attitudes on abortion, 60
  voting on abortion in legislatures, 96
public opinion
  and abortion rates, 6, 7, 10–11, 77–79,
    113–14, 116, 118–23, 130
  and access to abortion, 113–14, 116,
    118–23

and democratic theory 2–4, 127, 130
and policy, 1, 3–5, 9, 11, 75–76, 86–90,
  105–9, 112, 115–16, 118–23, 126–27,
  130
demographic factors influencing, 7–8,
  59–60, 79–84
omission from prior studies, 75–76
on abortion, 5, 7, 41–42, 59–74, 75–90,
  102–3, 105–9
on abortion in the fifty states, 78–79,
  102–3
policy moods, 5, 45
regression results, 81–85
stability of, 11, 61–67
surrogate measures of, 76

quasiexperimental designs, 47
Quinn, Bernard, 103

race and abortion attitudes, 60
Reagan, President Ronald
  Supreme Court appointments, 18, 20, 31
Reagan–Bush era, 46, 130
  impact on abortion rates, 48–49
Rehnquist, Chief Justice William, 15, 17,
  20, 21–22, 24, 26
  voting behavior in abortion cases,
    28–39
religion
  and abortion policies, 10–11, 103,
    105–9, 112, 116, 125
  and abortion rates, 116
  and support for abortion, 7, 10–11,
    59–60, 68–72, 79–84, 116, 125
  see also Catholics, fundamentalism,
    Jews, Mormons
religious intensity and abortion attitudes,
  68–72
representation, 3
research questions, 6–11
Rich, Richard, 6
Richard, Patricia, 101
RICO (Racketeering Influenced and
  Corrupt Organizations) Act, 26
Rockefeller, Governor Jay (WV), 90